HODSKINSON'S MAP OF SUFFOLK IN 1783

Introduction by D.P.Dymond

South West view of the Abbey Gate, Bury St Edmunds
Reproduced from the original map

THE
COUNTY
OF

By JOSEPH HODSKINSON,
of
Arundel Street, Strand.

LONDON:

Engraved and Published by WILLIAM FADEN, Geographer to the KING,

(Successor to Mr. Jefferys)

Charing Cross, August 14th. 1783.

Published by the Larks Press
Ordnance Farmhouse
Guist Bottom, Dereham
Norfolk NR20 5PF

01328 829207
Email: Larks.Press@btinternet.com
Website: www.booksatlarkspress.co.uk

Printed by the Lanceni Press
Garrood Drive, Fakenham, Norfolk
01328 851578

January 2003

ACKNOWLEDGEMENTS
Over a period of years we have been asked many times to produce an early map that would provide for the people of Suffolk something equivalent to the Larks Press editions of Faden's and Bryant's maps of Norfolk. In producing this edition of Hodskinson's map in book form, I am grateful to the Suffolk Record Society and to David Dymond for permission to reproduce his introduction, and for the latter's help with correcting the proofs. I must also thank the Suffolk Record Office's Ipswich branch for permission to reproduce their copy of the map (62494 FT37), and Doug Atfield for making the transparencies.
Finally, Peter and Susanna Wade-Martins were kind enough to lend me their copy of the Suffolk Record Society's edition of the map, which was a great help in the early stages of planning.
Susan Yaxley, Larks Press

British Library Cataloguing-in-Publication Data
A catalogue record for this book is available from the British Library

ISBN 1 904006 09 4

An Introduction to the Map

Written by D. P. Dymond in 1972 for the Suffolk Record Society's re-printing of the map, and slightly abbreviated for this edition.

Joseph Hodskinson's map of Suffolk was published on 14 August 1783.[1] In the following year it brought him a gold medal from the Royal Society for the Encouragement of Arts, Manufactures and Commerce.[2] At the time, compared with its many predecessors, it was by far the most detailed and accurate survey available. 'We esteem it here a very valuable acquisition' wrote Arthur Young from his home at Bradfield Combust.[3] For us today, its importance lies in the attempt to record the face of Suffolk before the pace of change rapidly accelerated in the nineteenth century. It came 42 years before the more consistent survey of C. and J. Greenwood (1825), and over 50 years before the Ordnance Survey printed its one-inch maps of the greater part of the county.[4] Although some early printed maps of Suffolk have been reproduced in modern times, this is the first re-issue of Hodskinson's map since its very limited second edition in 1820.[5] In spite of many defects, it is an historical document of considerable value which deserves to be better known and more widely used.

The original proposals for the survey were published in 1776, so the entire project from surveying to printing seems to have taken seven years. In comparison with the production of other eighteenth-century maps, this is a long time, but was certainly not unprecedented.[6] Revised proposals, which were printed in 1780 [Fig. 1], reveal that Hodskinson had started the work in partnership with another surveyor called A. Dury, but matters had been 'unavoidably retarded by the Death of the latter.'[7] The map was promised for April 1781 but further delays occurred. Yet another other target date, 1 May 1783, was passed[8] before the map finally appeared on 14 August 1783, at least three years later than originally intended.

The printed proposals were specifically aimed at the local nobility and gentry, in the hope that they would give advance subscriptions to help meet the costs of the survey. The price of the map was one-and-a-half guineas: one guinea to be paid in advance, and the remainder on delivery. In return the surveyor undertook to engrave the names of the subscribers 'at their Seats in the map'. No evidence has been found of the number of people employed by Hodskinson, or of the total sums of money involved in the project.[9] The publisher however was William Faden, Geographer to the King and one of the best-known names in English cartography.[10]

The original map was printed on six sheets of imperial paper, each with the main axis vertically or north-south. Surviving copies indicate that these sheets were usually trimmed, joined together, pasted to canvas, and kept either folded or on a large roller.[11] The full size of the printed surface when joined together is approximately 5 ft 3½ in by 3 ft 11 in.

The general appearance of the map is pleasing. The engraving is fine and well-balanced, and the varied lettering particularly attractive. Where there was space between the basic map and the rectangular frame, with its divisions of latitude and longitude, seven additions were fitted in. Across the top, moving left to right, are a triangulation diagram, a map of Ipswich (depicted as a ragged parchment, hanging, against the best archival practice, from three vicious-looking nails) and the title with imprint. At the bottom, moving left to right, are an engraving of the Abbey Gate at Bury (showing two houses, with a straight-joint between, abutting on the south), an 'Explanation' of conventions, a scale-bar, and finally Faden's dedication to the Duke of Grafton. In general terms, the map is remarkable for its straightforwardness and lack of embellishment: there are no decorative cartouches, heraldic designs or imaginative scenes with human figures, such as were used by other eighteenth-century cartographers. A few flourishes around certain words, particularly in the title and dedication, were quite sufficient as superficial decoration for Hodskinson and his publisher.

In the preparation of this edition, it soon

P R O P O S A L S

For Publiſhing by Subſcription,

A TOPOGRAPHICAL MAP

OF THE

COUNTY of *SUFFOLK*,

In SIX SHEETS of IMPERIAL PAPER,

On a SCALE of One INCH to a MILE:

IN WHICH WILL BE EXPRESSED

All the Main and Croſs Roads, Hills, Vallies, Rivers, Brooks, Ponds, Bridges, Mills, Woods, Heaths, Commons, Parks, Churches, Noblemen and Gentlemen's Seats, Houſes, Gardens, Cottages, and every Thing remarkable in the County, with the Diviſions of the Hundreds.

The ſame reduced on One Sheet, to ſerve as an INDEX to the Large One.

Surveyed by °JOSEPH HODSKINSON, *Arundel-Street, Strand.*

Printed for and publiſhed by WILLIAM FADEN, Succeſſor to the late *Thomas Jeffreys*, Geographer to the KING, the Corner of St. *Martin's Lane*, *Charing-Croſs*.

C O N D I T I O N S.

I. THE Subſcription is *One Guinea and an Half;* One Guinea to be paid at the Time of ſubſcribing, and the Remainder on Delivery of the Map; or, if it will be more ſatisfactory, Gentlemen may give only their Names and Addreſs, and pay the whole of the Subſcription when the Map is delivered.

II. The Noblemen's and Gentlemen's Names ſhall be engraved at their Seats in the Map.

III. The Names of Subſcribers ſhall be printed, as well as the Number of Maps they ſubſcribe for.

IV. The Map ſhall be well executed, and delivered in April, 1781.

*** *The above being the ſame Work which was begun ſome Time ſince by Meſſrs.* HODSKINSON *and* DURY, *but unavoidably retarded by the Death of the latter, Meſſrs.* HODSKINSON *and* FADEN *therefore beg Leave to acquaint thoſe Subſcribers, that their Subſcriptions will be allowed, and the Maps delivered as ſoon as publiſhed, agreeable to the Propoſals; and as they have undertaken to compleat and publiſh the above Survey at their own Riſk and Expence, they hope it will meet with the Patronage and Encouragement of the Nobility and Gentry of the County in general.*

March 30, 1780.

Subſcriptions are received by W. FADEN, the Corner of St. Martin's Lane, Charing-Croſs; J. HODSKINSON, Arundel-Street, Strand; or his Agents in the County; Mr. KENDALL, Printſeller, Bury St. Edmunds; Mr. PAGE, Bookſeller, at Ipſwich; and Mr. CHASE, Printer, at Norwich.

REceived of

the Sum of one Guinea, being the firſt Payment for the ſaid Map, which I promiſe to deliver on Payment of Half a Guinea more.

became apparent that there are considerable variations among surviving copies of the original map. Obviously some are cleaner and better preserved than others, but there are also differences in the intensity of the inking, particularly towards the edges of the constituent sheets. Furthermore all the copies inspected had been hand-coloured in some way, either by picking out details such as hundred-boundaries, built-up areas, major roads and parkland, or by an overall colour-wash which distinguishes the hundreds. In fact, a copy in the Suffolk Record Office at Ipswich has been used for this reproduction.[12]

The Survey

Here we have the advantage of an inset triangulation diagram which shows the 'principal Stations' or major surveying points, and the angles between them (see sheet I).[13] Some 38 points are shown within the county, and three outside (at Ely, Cambs., Croxton, Norfolk, and near Bulmer, Essex - this last is unlabelled). Curiously, although these are distributed fairly evenly over the greater part of the map, there are areas apparently not covered (e.g. around Newmarket and Haverhill, and above all the north-eastern corner roughly from Halesworth up to the tip of Lothingland). One can offer no obvious explanation for these gaps: the topography is not particularly difficult and there is no lack of suitable landmarks. The triangulation diagram may well show an original and incomplete pattern which was subsequently extended. Most of the points are in parishes on comparatively high ground, with fair visibility in several directions, such as Otley, Somerton and Bedfield. A check on the angles given confirms that most of the sightings were taken from churches, presumably from the western towers. In a comparatively gentle landscape like Suffolk's, and given clear atmospheric conditions, it is astonishing how far one can often see from towers 50 to 100 feet high. Other kinds of building were used where appropriate, for example a windmill at Levington and the castle at Orford. In the case of St. Edmund's Hill, to the east of Bury, a purely natural eminence is specified, but even here it is certain from the bearings that the roof of Mr Symonds' house, now Morton Hall, was used. Lines of sight connect those points which were apparently inter-visible on the ground, and form, in Hodskinson's words, 'a Series of Triangles continued throughout the County'.[14] Some of these lines are over considerable distances, for instance from Croxton to Barrow (15.3 miles) and from Cransford to Dunwich (10.75 miles), but it is important to remember that theodolites with telescopic sights were available by this date. On the other hand, it is sometimes surprising that places fairly close together were not apparently inter-visible (e.g. Occold and Stradbroke, only 5.13 miles apart). One imagines that some of these sightings were taken in the winter, because the foliage of trees, shown in great numbers on large-scale manuscript maps, would have cut down visibility at any other season.[15] Hodskinson seems to have given his bearings to the nearest minute. When fifty of these were roughly checked against a modern one-inch map, the vast majority seemed to be accurate and confirmed many of the survey-points.[16] However there were areas where one suspects the bearings to be wrong (e.g. around Bacton, Elmswell, Stonham [Aspal] and Stowmarket).

Only two linear measurements are shown on this inset map: 6½ miles from Barrow church to St. Edmund's Hill, and 7,760½ yards from the windmill on Levington Heath to Rushmore [*sic*]. One might assume that these are the base-lines from which Hodskinson built up his triangulations, but they are both of very questionable accuracy. To get a precise horizontal measurement, the first line is a curious choice as it crosses major obstacles like the town of Bury, as well as considerable natural undulations like the Lark valley. In view of the difficulties, one cannot be surprised at the imprecision of the measurement. In fact the true horizontal measurement between these two points seems to be 6.83 miles. The second, shorter line to the south-east of Ipswich was measured across flatter country, which was mainly open heath at the time. At first it seems significant that the distance is given to the nearest half-yard rather than half-mile, but again a serious discrepancy needs to be explained. Whereas the bearings suggest that 'Rushmore' is Rushmere St. Andrew church, the measurement given is nowhere near the true distance from Levington windmill, which is 8,200 yards.[17] So far as the triangulation diagram indicates, Hodskinson did not lay out a base-line along a length of beach or foreshore, which was the normal method of obtaining a carefully measured horizontal measurement easily adjusted to mean sea-level.

On the basis of his triangulated framework, Hodskinson claimed that the roads, buildings and other details were 'actually Surveyed & truly delineated.'[18] No doubt considerable attention was paid at this stage to the recording of linear features like roads and streams. We have no evidence of the instruments used, but among those available were theodolites and circumferentors (for measuring angles), chains, perambulators, and pedometers (for linear measurements) as well as the plane-table which enables surveyors to produce scale-drawings in the field.[19]

The Scale

We know nothing about the scale at which Hodskinson and his staff worked in the field and on preliminary drawings, but the published version, like many other county maps in the eighteenth century, was at the scale of one inch to a mile.[20] One earlier printed map of Suffolk had already achieved this scale, John Kirby's of 1736 (2nd edition, 1766), but this was considerably less accurate and detailed. Arthur Young had dismissed it, perhaps rather uncharitably, as 'a miserable one'.[21] On Hodskinson's map, the two inset-maps of Ipswich and the survey-framework have very different scales: the first is 1 inch to *c.* 120 yards, and has its own scale-bar and the second is 1 inch to *c.* 4.4 miles. It is also worth mentioning here that in 1787 Faden produced a smaller, simplified version of Hodskinson's map, at the scale of ½ inch to a mile.[22]

Conventions

The conventions used are normal for the late eighteenth century. In the bottom-left corner of the map, Hodskinson appended an 'Explanation' or key which listed them rather inadequately. Four kinds of script are employed: roman capitals for the names of market towns; roman upper-and-lower case for the names of parishes; italic upper-and-lower case for all other topographical names (e.g. halls, woods and greens); and a light sloping copper-plate for personal names.

Two symbols are shown for churches and chapels; they are small elevational drawings of a church, with or without a spire capping the western tower (e.g. Rattlesden, Swilland and Sibton are among the few with spires). Gentlemen's seats or 'noted Houses' are shown as small elevational drawings, usually with one to three chimneys and cross-wings. Watermills are shown as circular symbols with rays; windmills are shown by small elevational drawings of a post-mill. All other kinds of buildings, including farms, cottages and out-buildings are shown in plan as rectangular black blocks. Parks are heavily stippled with a bounding symbol representing the pale or fence.

Roads are shown by double lines, solid where the road is enclosed by hedges and pecked where the road is crossing open country (heaths, fens, greens or, as between Mildenhall and West Row, open arable fields). Along the main roads are marked turnpikes, milestones and mileages from either local towns or London. Bridges are simply shown as the continuation of roads over rivers and streams: some, both major and minor, are labelled; others, both major and minor, are not. A few causeways across marshland are labelled, for example, Latymere Dam near Kessingland.

Hodskinson, like most surveyors of his time, shows the major administrative boundaries of the shire and its constituent hundreds. When these are not following some major natural feature like a river or the coast, they are shown as a dot-dash line for the shire, and a pecked line for the hundred; overall these boundaries are fortified by hand-painted lines of colour.[23]

There are several symbols representing details of the physical landscape. All large stretches of water, whether rivers, estuaries, decoys or the sea, are shown by solid lines for the bank or coast and a series of fine engraved lines for the water, getting progressively lighter as they move out from the land: the total effect is of a delicate kind of shading. Narrow streams are indicated by a single solid line.

All kinds of uncultivated land (greens, commons, heaths, fens or coastal marshes) are shown by a pecked overall symbol or horizontal shading, both representing rough grass. A symbol representing a tree in elevation is also used intermittently to denote scrub. The same symbol filling complete areas represents woodland proper.[24]

Finally, Hodskinson employed the usual

delicate shading of his period to show relief. The darker end of the shading represents the higher end of the slope, as if the sun were falling on the uplands and casting deep shadows on the slopes. This convention has particularly emphasized the valleys, even some of the slightest (see the Hawstead area, south of Bury). On the coastal Sandlings and the Breckland, one's attention is drawn more towards blocks of 'upland'. Although this kind of symbol gives no notion of actual or relative height, it does convey, in a landscape where the main elevational features are valleys cut into extensive plateaux, a fair impression of the shape of the land.

The County Boundary *c.* 1780

There are eight noteworthy differences between the county boundary then and now. (1) In the north-west corner, a sizeable chunk of fenland was then included within Suffolk, which is now part of Cambridgeshire and Norfolk. This is the area within the confluence of the rivers Great and Little Ouse, and bounded by Brandon Creek, Littleport Bridge and Prickwillow. (2) Thetford south of the Little Ouse was then counted as Suffolk, not Norfolk as now. (3) Half of the town of Harleston was then included within Suffolk, with the boundary down the centre of the main street. This is the result of the anomalous position of Mendham since at least Domesday times: this parish was 'situated on both sides of the River Waveney, taking into its Bounds Part of the Town of Harleston'.[25] (4) Gorleston is shown as part of Suffolk (it was transferred to Norfolk in 1891). (5) Ballingdon on the south bank of the River Stour, opposite Sudbury, was not then included within Suffolk. (6) There are minor differences in the vicinity of Haverhill and Sturmer (Essex). (7) The boundary then ran down the main street of Newmarket, dividing St. Mary's parish in Suffolk from All Saints' in Cambridgeshire: this boundary was not down the middle of the road as at Harleston, but close to the frontage on the south (Cambridgeshire) side, thus necessitating the hinged shop-signs which Richard Blome described in 1673.[26] (8) Where the boundary today takes in a rectangle on the left bank of the River Kennett near Freckenham, Hodskinson shows it following the river without deviation.

The Reliability and Historical uses of the Map

Although the Royal Society of Arts accepted the map as 'accurately laid down and neatly executed', and Arthur Young was able to say that it was 'very correct in all places that I have yet particularly examined',[27] we are forced to ask just how good it is by modern standards, and therefore how informative it is of Suffolk in the period 1776-83. When the overall accuracy of the map was crudely tested by measuring two long lines across the county, one roughly east-west and the other north-south, it was found in each case that Hodskinson's distance was an underestimate of the true distance by three to four per cent.[28] When three lengths from Hodskinson's triangulation framework were similarly tested, it was found that he had again underestimated the true distance, this time by an average of 2.7 per cent.[29] Distortion is also reflected in the latitudes and longitudes given on the map. Fourteen points throughout the county were checked. In latitude, Hodskinson shows all of them to the north of their true positions, though by varying distances. In longitude, the contraction of the county mentioned above is confirmed by the fact that points in the western and central parts of the county (e.g. Littleport Bridge and Stowmarket church) are shown to the east of their true positions, while those in the eastern parts (e.g. Snape Bridge and the mouth of Oulton Dyke) are shown to the west of their true positions.

On the whole the outline of the county is shown adequately, and can easily be identified by reference to the modern one-inch map. Where the boundary has frequent minor irregularities, these tend to get smoothed out (e.g. to the west of Lidgate). More important, there are places where the true shape of the boundary has been seriously distorted (e.g. at the north end of Exning parish).

The hundred boundaries are clearly unreliable: they are highly simplified and approximate, with many suspicious-looking straight lengths and regular curves which are quite unlike most ancient boundaries in the county. They are only a slight improvement on the days of Saxton and Speede, and were done on the basis of minimal survey and research. For example, at Bedingfield Hodskinson implausibly suggests that the boundary slashed right across the parish: the church is shown in Hoxne Hundred and Bedingfield Green in Hartismere! If this map is to be used as evidence for changes in the hundred boundaries, then it must be related to other more reliable sources.

The internal reliability of the map is clearly variable, and ranges from poor to excellent. In most areas where some sort of check is possible with a near-contemporary manuscript map, it seems that the general pattern of settlement is represented fairly well, but there are frequent discrepancies and many buildings are not shown at all. For example, comparison with a manuscript map of Benacre in 1778[30] shows the omission of several houses along the street to the east of the church. Bearing in mind how eighteenth-century surveyors relied on road-traverses, it is perhaps not surprising that a high number of isolated farms have been omitted, such as Hall Farm, Great Ashfield (a moated farmstead, clearly shown on an estate map of 1773), Chapel Farm, Hitcham (a partially sixteenth-century building) and Impaugh Farm, Stonham Aspal (a medieval structure).[31] What is less forgiveable is that sometimes whole groups of houses are totally omitted: e.g. a small hamlet of timber-framed buildings in Rougham (Grid Ref. TL 895628); a straggle of houses to the west of Holton Hall, near Hadleigh; or, strangely, the houses on each side of outer Southgate Street and St John's Street, Bury.[32] The rectangular blocks which Hodskinson uses for most buildings seem to agree in most cases with the evidence of manuscript maps only in so far as *general* siting is concerned, and there are frequent discrepancies in the finer points of siting and orientation.[33] Where two or more of these symbols are shown close together, they usually represent a farmhouse with its barn and other out-buildings. However, one cannot assume that, for every house shown, the barn is necessarily included: Hodskinson tends to show the barns which are beside the larger and more important farms, but there must be scores which he omits.

In spite of all the defects mentioned above, this map gives, for the majority of Suffolk parishes and towns, the first impression we have in map-form of the pattern of settlement. It therefore has a lot to tell the critical topographical historian: the shape and size of hamlets, villages and towns; the existence of some isolated farms and cottages; and the rough balance between nucleation and dispersal in different parts of the county. This kind of information is all the more valuable in rural parishes if there has been subsequent desertion (e.g. Slaughden), shrinkage (e.g. Wangford, near Lakenheath), or expansion (e.g. Reydon, near Southwold), or where towns have subsequently expanded (e.g. Lowestoft).

Hodskinson, mindful of 'the Patronage and Encouragement of the Nobility and Gentry of the County', has given us an important record of the principal seats and parks, and has indicated most of the owners (see Proposals of 1780, Fig. 1). The houses themselves are shown rather conventionally, but the parks were individually surveyed. Much internal detail is depicted, such as carriage-drives, enclosed gardens, lakes with islands, tree-avenues, blocks of woodland and even, it seems, a prospect-mound (at Livermere Parva).

One must certainly not forget the value of many of the place-names. Several hamlets, for instance, have apparently been re-named since 1783 (e.g. Mill Green, Stonham Aspal was then Northern Green). The map also enables the local historian to identify at least one lost settlement: Kelton Green, now part of Benhall Street, is clearly the missing Domesday 'vill' of *Keletuna* or *Chiletuna.*[34] Furthermore, individual buildings in special categories are sometimes named: apart from the numerous Halls, there are the economically-important warren lodges (see the Breckland parishes), Houses of Industry and the occasional pest-house (see Mendlesham and Halesworth). On the other hand, it must be recognized that some of Hodskinson's place-names are corruptions: for example he marks the hamlet of Bridge Street, north of Long Melford, as *Bread* Street.

On the whole, Hodskinson seems to have made a determined and reasonably successful attempt to portray the tight, intricate road-pattern of Suffolk. No doubt the plane-tabling, measurement and drawing of this detail took a great deal of time. All the major roads are shown, and the majority of the minor ones. Many hedged lanes on the map have now entirely disappeared, or simply survive as rights of way across featureless ploughland. The accuracy is also sufficient for the historian to spot where some re-alignment has taken place since *c.* 1780 (e.g. on the main Ipswich-Norwich road, by Westwick Farm, Thornham Magna). The occasional name applied to a road has special interest (e.g. the Packways in Henstead and Kelsale, and the Old London Road at Elveden).

This map is the best record the economic historian has of the distribution of ancient common land in the county. Although much arable and meadow, particularly in High Suffolk, had been enclosed centuries before, and although local people had been converting bits of common land into private property since at least the thirteenth century, there was still a substantial acreage of greens, commons and heaths for Hodskinson to record in 1783.[35] Recent fieldwork in the Rougham area has shown that he depicted these features with commendable accuracy, even down to quite small-scale details.[36] This may well be a reflection of the increasing contemporary interest in the possibilities of enclosing the remaining 'waste'. Hodskinson's map and Arthur Young's *General View of the Agriculture of Suffolk* (1797) must surely have contributed to the general acceptance of this idea, certainly among the propertied classes, by stressing the acreage and distribution of various kinds of common land. In the next 50 years, a spate of Acts and private agreements were to transform most of the commons into totally private property.[37]

The peculiar value of the map is the careful *outline* it usually gives for each common. On the ground this outline was of course a ditch and hedge, which are often noticeably more massive than others in the locality. When the boundaries of ancient commons can still be identified (after about 150 years of enclosure), then they are among the most precious features in our landscape, and surely deserve protection for their historical and biological interest.[38] It is also worth comment that a number of post-mills stood within or beside the commons (e.g. Mellis and Barking Tye). Nor should we forget the other kind of common land, the marshland and fens of the valleys and coast, which were also in many cases to be drained and enclosed in the nineteenth century. Witness for example the fascinating pattern of marshland in Carlton Colville (west of Lowestoft), with its water-courses, causeways and partial encroachments, or the now-vanished 'broads' between Kessingland and Minsmere.

Woodland by contrast is not one of Hodskinson's successes. Most woods are depicted as rather indistinct blobs, which do not often correspond in detail to their historical shapes as known from boundary-earthworks, maps and written documents. For example, the outline of Hintlesham Great and Ramsey Woods, east of Hadleigh, is wildly inaccurate when compared to maps of 1595, 1721 and 1838.[39] Nevertheless Hodskinson at least indicates the existence of many woods. At Wattisham, as a random example, he shows a large area of woodland (East and Deer Woods) which is not indicated by the Greenwoods in 1825.

Hodskinson also includes a certain amount of antiquarian information. Unlike Bowen (1750) he has no special symbols for religious houses and castles, but he does at least label the latter. He indicates churches and chapels which were 'in ruins' (e.g. Hazlewood and Thorpe, both near Aldeburgh, and Eriswell near Lakenheath). Some 'barrows' or burial-mounds are also shown by a shaded circular symbol, e.g. near Icklingham and Nacton. To the north of Bury is shown the mound of Thingoe, where the hundred court met in early medieval times, but it is not labelled in any way.

Compared with Yates' Lancashire (1786) and Donn's Devon (1765), this map unfortunately carries only a small amount of detail concerning industrial and commercial life.[40] Apart from the mills, this is mainly connected with water-transport (e.g. locks and 'stanches' along rivers, the old and new 'keys' near Southwold, the lighthouse at Lowestoft and the beacons on Orford Ness), but reference to local brick-making is occasionally made (e.g. Stowlangtoft and Westleton).

The inset map of Ipswich is merely a simplification of Joseph Pennington's large-scale printed map of the town, which had appeared in 1778.[41] This is a good example of the copying and re-drawing which were so common among early cartographers.

How then can we sum up the value of Hodskinson's map? In spite of many defects which the critical historian must never ignore, it is an indispensable control or framework for the topographical history of Suffolk, for it gives us the best impression we have of the traditional patterns of the county, to a large extent medieval in origin, before the impact in the nineteenth century of greater industrialization, accelerated population growth and improved communications.

Joseph Hodskinson

No details are known of his birth, but when he married Ann Haynes at St. George's, Bloomsbury in 1770, he was described as 'aged thirty Years and upwards'.[42] He died, probably in London, between February 1811 and February 1812.[43] Like so many men of his period, Hodskinson appears to have had wide interests, professional and otherwise. At first he seems to have concentrated on engraving, but soon established a reputation as a land-surveyor. At various times during his life, he was also styled architect, engineer and publisher. Appropriately he became a member of that remarkably polymath institution, the Royal Society for the Encouragement of Arts, etc., which had been founded in London in 1754.[44] From at least 1784, his business (known latterly as Joseph Hodskinson and Co., Surveyors) was based at 34-5 Arundel Street, the Strand, London.[45]

Hodskinson was involved in the production of at least four printed surveys of English counties. In addition to his medal-winning map of Suffolk (1783), he was engraver of a map of Bedfordshire (1765), engraver and co-publisher of a map of Cumberland (1774), and co-surveyor of Yorkshire (1771-2).[46] Between 1774 and 1786 he exhibited drawings, including original architectural designs, at both the Free Society of Artists and the Royal Academy.[47] He also wrote two short books on farm management, drainage and road-improvement, produced several reports and plans on major engineering works (including the famous Eau Brink cut, near King's Lynn), designed several houses and produced a number of manuscript surveys.

Hodskinson's Printed Works

The Report of Joseph Hodskinson, Engineer, respecting the State of Wells Harbour, in the County of Norfolk......(1782, London)
A Plan and Estimates for Improving the Navigation of the River Stour, County Kent......(1792, Canterbury)
Report...on the probable effect which a New Cut, now in contemplation from Eau Brink to a little above Lynn, will have on the Harbour & Navigation of Lynn......(1793, London)
Plain and Useful Instructions to Farmers, or An Improved Method of Management of Arable Land with some hints upon Drainage and the Improvement of Turnpike and Cross Roads......(1794, London)
The Farmer's Guide, or An Improved Method of Management of Arable Land...(1794, London)

Hodskinson's Surveys *(excluding county maps)*

1773, estate at Bedington, Surrey; with plan of house assumed to be also by Hodskinson (Surrey CRO: 173/3/6a-b)
1774, estate of Lord Romney in Cuxton and Halling, Kent (Kent Archives Office: CCRb P1)
1778, estates of the Duke of Norfolk in Sussex (Arundel Castle MSS: RL 5) s.d., Arundel and adjoining lands, Sussex (Arundel Castle MSS: LM 20)
1779, Hempsted estate in nine parishes in Kent and Sussex (a volume of twenty maps, Kent Archives Office: U78 P27)
1779, titheable lands in the Hempsted estate, Benenden, Kent (volume of eight maps, Kent Archives Office: U78 P36)
1781, manors of Moulsey Matham and Moulsey Prior, Surrey (Surrey CRO: 81/3/1; copy of 1798 in PRO: MR 293)
1783, manor of Dorking, Surrey, redrawn from earlier survey of 1649 (Arundel Castle MSS: LM9)
1785, estate at Ravensden, Bedfordshire (Bedfordshire CRO: X1/21)
1785-6, manor of Kennington by Middleton and Hodskinson (Duchy of Cornwall records)
1789, Cheshire estates of Earl of Shrewsbury (copy, 1798, of survey and valuation by Hill and Hodskinson, 1789, Arundel Castle MSS: RB5)
1789, Burghfield estate, Berkshire, of Earl of Shrewsbury (copy, 1797, of survey and valuation by Hill and Hodskinson, 1789, Arundel Castle MSS: RB5)
1789, two plans of Burghfield estate, Berkshire; although unsigned, Hodskinson could have done one or both (Arundel Castle MSS: TP 35 and 36)
1790, estate at Huddington, Worcestershire (BM: MAPS C.7.e.16 (7))
1794, the River Thames from London Bridge to the King's mooring chains at Deptford (printed map, from *Report of....the Port of London,* Appendix P)
1811, intended improvement, New Shoreham harbour, Sussex; accompanied by book of reference and estimates also by Hodskinson (West Sussex CRO: QDP/W 25)
1822, the parish of St Mary, Kensington, including Old and New Brompton, and north side of Little Chelsea; by Bassett, Christian and Hodskinson [probably Joseph Hodskinson, though he had died 1811-12] (Kensington and Chelsea Central Library)

There must be other examples of Hodskinson's work which are not listed above. The writer of this introduction would be interested to know of these.

Acknowledgements

The writer would like to thank W.R. Serjeant, T. James, J. Todd, N. Scarfe and J. Campbell for valuable help and advice in the preparation of the map, Mrs J. Buck for her kindness in searching out details of Hodskinson's life, R.H. Fairclough, Dr J.B. Harley and Dr P. Eden for useful criticisms of this introduction, and D.G.C. Allan, Curator-Librarian of the Royal Society of Arts for permission to use the Society's records. Finally I wish to acknowledge the unfailing co-operation of many archivists and librarians, unfortunately too numerous to name individually, and the interest shown by the staff of W. S. Cowell Ltd.

References

Abbreviations: RSA: Royal Society of Arts
SROB: Suffolk Record Office (Bury St Edmunds branch)
SROI: Suffolk Record Office (Ipswich branch)

1. The date is given on the margins of some constituent sheets. See unjoined copy, Bodleian Library: Gough maps, Suffolk 16.
2. *Trans. RSA,* III (1785), p. 181. For the influence of the Society in fostering surveys of English counties, see J. B. Harley, *Jour. RSA,* CXII, pp. 43, 119, 269 & 538.
3. RSA Manuscript Transactions, 1783-4, No. 14: letter of 22 December, 1783.
4. C. & J. Greenwood, *Map of the County of Suffolk from an Actual Survey made in the Years 1823 & 1824* (published 1825). The one-inch OS maps of the greater part of Suffolk were published 1836-8, but two Essex sheets, which included a strip of southern Suffolk, had appeared as early as 1805.
5. I am indebted to R.H. Fairclough of the Map Room, Cambridge Univ. Lib. for pointing out the 2nd ed. of 1820 (copy in CUL, Maps b.86.82.3); the only alterations made to the plates concern the names of landowners (e.g. at Redgrave, Adm[ira]l Wilson has replaced Rowland Holt Esq.; at Woolverston, Chas. Berners Esqr. has replaced Wm. Berners Esq.). Dr Harley has also reminded me that there could be other states of the plate between 1783 and 1820.
6. No copy of the original proposals of 1776 has been found, but they are mentioned in Rich. Gough, *British Topography* (1780), Vol. 2, p. 258. For the amount of time spent on county surveys, see J.B. Harley, *op. cit.,* pp. 45, 120 & 540. Day's map of Somerset also took seven years to complete.
7. Bodleian Library, Oxford: Gough, General Topography 365, interleaved between pages 258 and 259. The facsimile is reproduced by permission of the Curators of the Bodleian Library. No copy of the index-map mentioned in the 1780 proposals has been found.
8. *Bury and Norwich Post,* 20 March 1783, and subsequently.
9. There seem to be about 150 names of subscribers on the map, which implies an income from sales of at least £236 5s 0d. Yet the costs of such surveys could run into thousands of pounds: see J.B. Harley, *Imago Mundi,* XIX (1965) p. 63.
10. See Map Collectors Circle reprint (1963) of *Catalogue of the Geographical Works, Maps, Plans, &c. Published by W. Faden, 5, Charing Cross*...1822.
11. There are originals in SROB (578/1, folded in original box; 279/32, rolled); SROI (Acc. 1590, rolled; HA 11/E1/2, rolled); and Ipswich Borough Lib. (folded copy). Others are mentioned in E.M. Rodger, *Large-scale county maps of the Brit. Isles* 1596-1850 (1960)
12. SROI, Acc: 1590. (There is another good copy with a minimum of tinting in the BM, K.39.7.8 TAB.END.)
13. See J.B. Harley, *Imago Mundi,* XIX (1965), p. 56 for mention of the minority of county surveyors who included triangulation diagrams.
14. RSA Manuscript Transactions, 1783-4, No. 14: letter of 26 November, 1783.
15. E.g. in SROB, E3/10/10.2: survey of Badwell Ash Farm (Badwell Hall) in 1762. On 216 acres, about 690 trees in hedgerows and meadows, mostly pollards, were recommended for felling, so that 'the many hundreds' left could be properly managed.
16. Churches were used at Croxton, Ingham, Stanton St. John, Elmswell, Bradfield St. George, Bacton, Burgate, Occold, Otley, Pettistree, Tunstall, Waldringfield and no doubt in many other parishes. 'Freshore' seems to be Freston church.
17. The site of Levington windmill can be readily identified on large-scale OS maps.
18. RSA Manuscript Transactions, 1783-4, No. 14: letter of 26 November, 1783.
19. See W.L.D. Ravenhill, introduction to *Benjamin Donn, a map of the County of Devon,* 1765. (Devon & Cornwall Rec. Soc., 1965), pp. 8-11; also J.B. Harley, introduction to *William Yates's map of Lancashire,* 1786 (Historic Soc. of Lancs. & Cheshire, 1968), pp. 12-13.
20. Actually, because of the shrinkage of the paper, the scale is slightly *under* one inch to a mile.
21. RSA Manuscript Transactions, 1783-4, No. 14: letter of 22 December, 1783. There are considerable differences between the 1736 & 1766 editions of

Kirby's map. Locally, copies of the 1736 map are rare.
22. *The County of Suffolk Reduced from the Large Map in Six Sheets Surveyed by Joseph Hodskinson...Printed for Willm. Faden,...Jany 1st,* 1787.
23. The first printed map of the county to show *parish* boundaries is C. & J. Greenwood (1825).
24. Unfortunately no attempt is made by Hodskinson to depict field-systems.
25. J. Kirby, *Suffolk Traveller* (1764) p. 168. See also H.C. Darby, *Domesday Geography of Eastern England* (1952), p. 101.
26. R. Blome, *Britannia* (1673), p. 211: '...but their Market-place and whole street is in Suffolk, which occasions those that live on the South-side to hang all their Signposts on hinges, so that when the fancy takes them, they may draw them to the sides of the Wall, and consequently into their own County.'
27. RSA Minutes of Committees, 1783-4, pp. 96-97: meeting of Polite Arts committee, 13 January, 1784; RSA Manuscript Transactions, 1783-4, No. 14: letter of 22 December, 1783.
28. The distance between Minsmere Haven and the confluence of the rivers Kennett and Lark is 51.25 miles; on Hodskinson's map this distance is given (making allowance for shrinkage) as 49.4 miles. Similarly the distance between the confluence of the Dove and Waveney and that of the Brett and Stour is 28.7 miles; Hodskinson renders it 27.8 miles.
29. These lines were Barrow church to Levington windmill, Occold to Stoke [by Nayland], and Lavenham to Metfield.
30. SROI, T 631.
31. Map of estate at Ashfield, SROI, AE: 153/5. For Impaugh Farm, see Penrose and Hill, 'The houses of Stonham Aspal', *Suffolk Review,* Vol. 4, pp. 39-44.
32. For estate in Holton and surrounding parishes, 1779, see SROB E3/5/3; for Bury, see Thos. Warren's survey of 1791.
33. E.g. compare Hodskinson with a map of Fiske's Farm, Norton, 1785: SROI, T4/31/5.1.
34. *ex inf.* Norman Scarfe. See his *The Suffolk Landscape* (1972) pp.174-7 and *VCH Suffolk,* Vol. 1, pp. 447 and 466.
35. For thirteenth-century encroachments on road-verges and commons, see *Rotuli Hundredorum,* Vol. II (1818), pp. 182-200, under 'purprestures'. Wetheringsett Green is a classic example, physically, of early piecemeal enclosure. Arthur Young thought that over 100,000 acres of 'waste' were still left in Suffolk in 1794 (*Gen. View of the Agriculture of...Suffolk,* p. 19).
36. Unpublished fieldwork by C.R. Ranson and D.P. Dymond.
37. See W.E. Tate, 'A Handlist of Suffolk Enclosure Acts and Awards', *Proc. Suff. Inst. of Arch.,* XXV (1952), pp. 225-263; Thirsk and Imray, *Suffolk Farming in the 19th century* (1958), pp. 60-3. It is ironic that the 2nd edition of Hodskinson's map virtually ignored the enclosures that had occurred, and showed the commons as they had been about 40 years earlier.
38. See M.D. Hooper, W.G. Hoskins *et alia, Hedges and Local History* (Standing Conf. on Local Hist., 1971).
39. The 1595 and 1721 maps of Hintlesham are reproduced in G.H. Ryan and L.J. Redstone, *Timperley of Hintlesham* (1931); for OS one-inch of 1838, see David and Charles reprint, sheet 64. A recent attempt by Mr J. Knox to read significance into the shape of Felsham Hall and Monkspark Woods, six miles S.E. of Bury, as given by Hodskinson, Greenwood (1825) and Bryant (1826), has only proved the inaccuracy and contradictoriness of these maps for woodland shapes and areas (*East Anglian Daily Times,* 10 Feb., 1972).
40. W.L.D. Ravenhill (Ed.), *Benjamin Donn, A Map of the County of Devon,* 1765 (Devon & Cornwall Rec. Soc., 1965); J.B. Harley (ed.) *William Yates's map of Lancashire,* 1786 (Historic Soc. of Lancs. & Cheshire, 1968).
41. Joseph Pennington, *A Map of the Town of Ipswich...finished* 1778.
42. Bish. of London's Registry, marriage alleg. & bond, 20 July 1770; GLC Record Office, register of St George's, Bloomsbury, 22 July 1770. His family was probably Lancastrian in origin. Most of Hodskinson's wealth, as shown in his will, consisted of properties in the Aldgate, Southwark and Strand areas of London.
43. PRO, PCC wills, PROB.11, 1530/77: registered copy of Hodskinson's will dated 5 February, 1811, proved 27 February, 1812.
44. *Trans. RSA,* Vol. 1 (1783), list of contributing members.
45. E.g. *Holden's Triennial Directory 1805, 1806 and 1807.*
46. E.M. Rodger, *Large-scale county maps of the Brit. Isles 1596-1850* (1960).
47. Algernon Graves, *The Royal Academy of Arts, Complete Dictionary of Contributors...1769-1904* (1906); *The Free Society of Artists 1761-83: a Complete Dictionary of Contributors...*(1907).

Market Towns in Capitals, . as...... CLARE

Parishes in Print.................as....... Claydon

Churches or Chapels...........................

Seats or noted Houses.................

Parks...........................

Inclosed Roads..................

Open Roads......................

Rivers, Brooks & Hills..........

Farms or Cottages.....................

NOTE: readers should be aware of the following points:

a) The original map, mounted on canvas, was folded; the folds have opened, introducing horizontal and vertical gaps which are visible on this photographic copy.

b) The original map consisted of six large sheets of paper (imperial size, 30 by 22 ins); where it has been necessary to piece together sections of different sheets to provide overlap, the joins between them are also visible on this copy, sometimes with slight but unavoidable distortion.

c) The broad dark lines on this copy mark the boundaries of administrative hundreds, and were hand-painted in colour on the original.

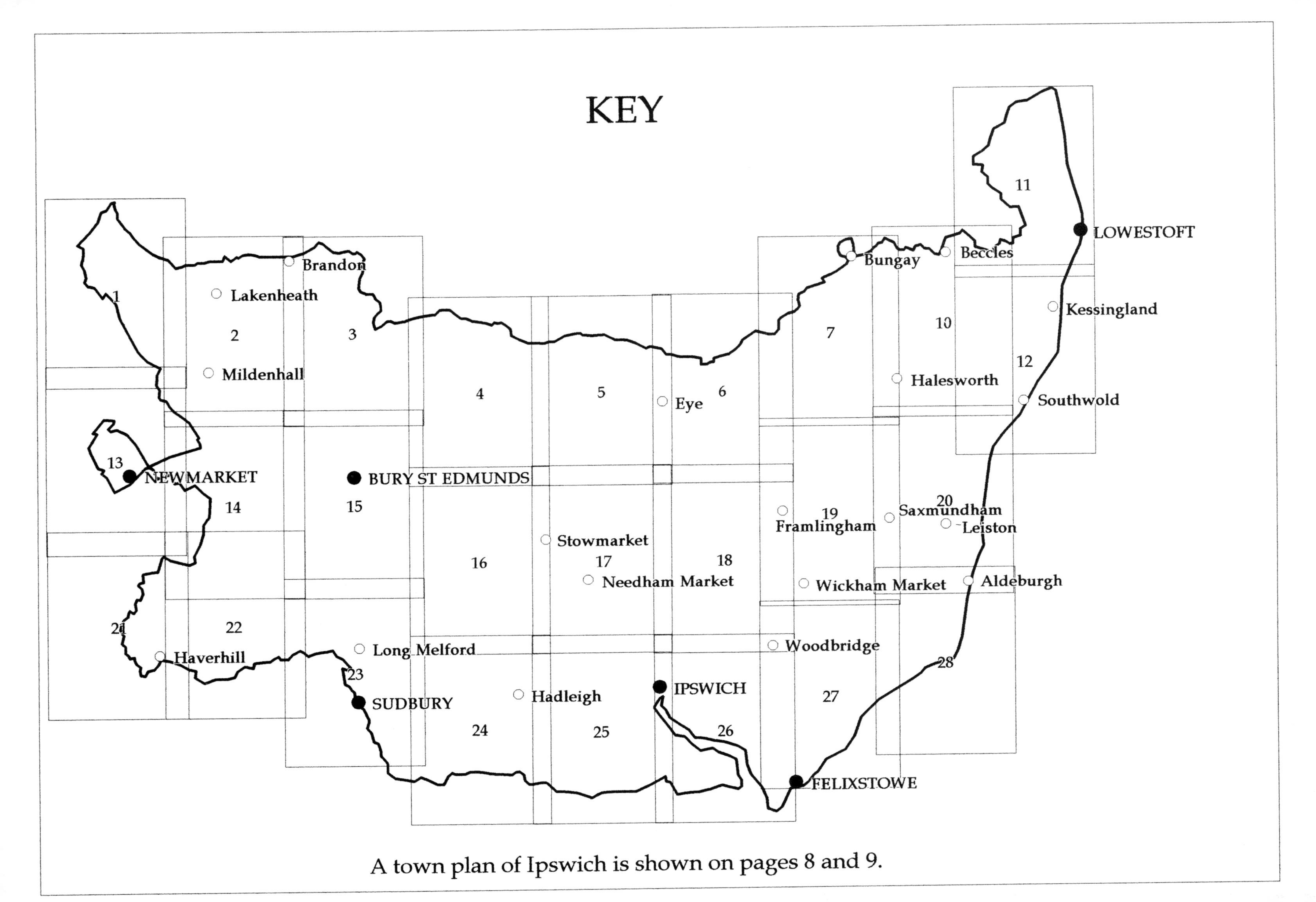

A town plan of Ipswich is shown on pages 8 and 9.

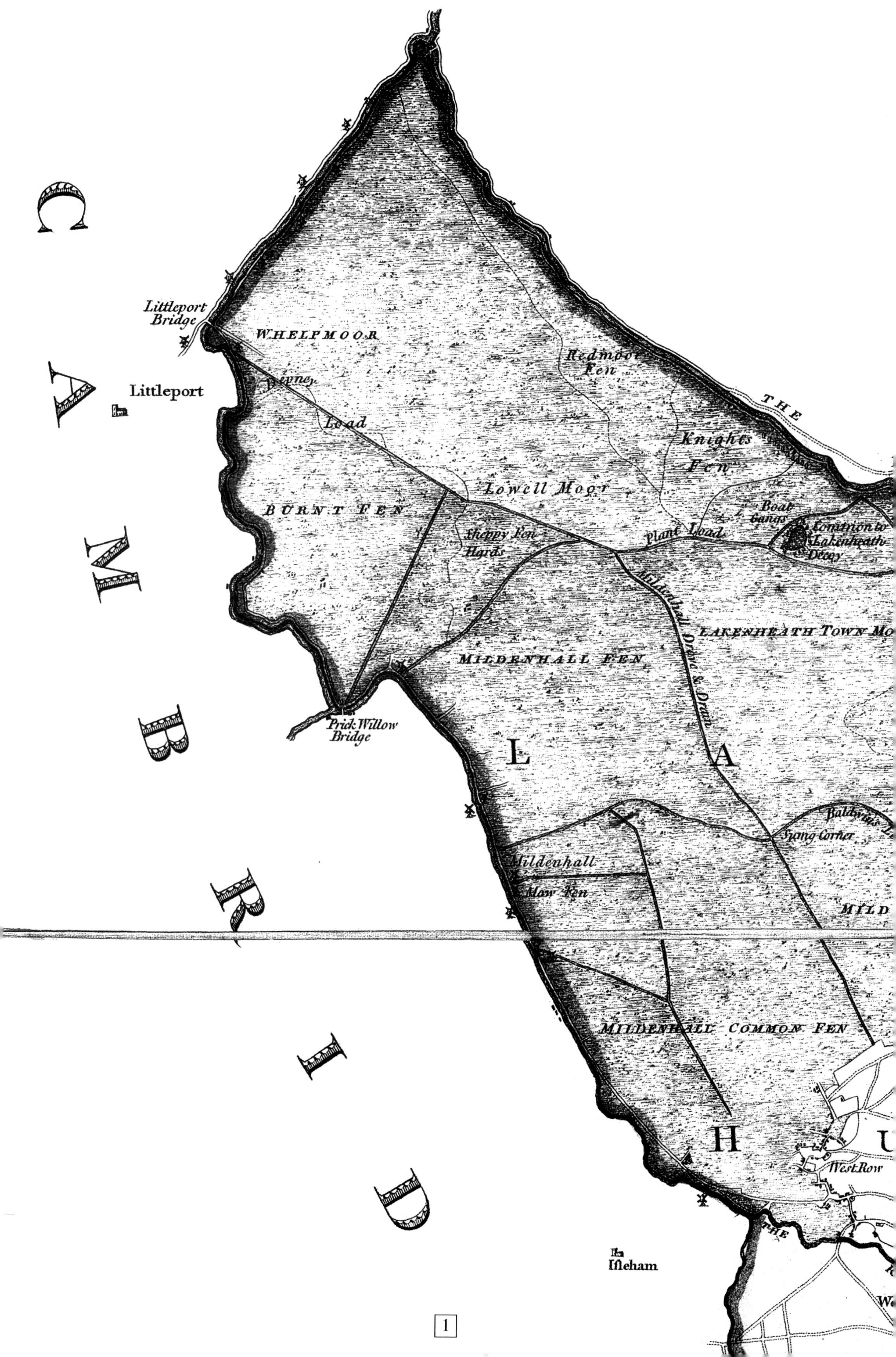
C A M B R I D
Littleport Bridge
Littleport
WHELPMOOR
Redmoor Fen
THE
Load
Knights Fen
Lowell Moor
BURNT FEN
Boat Gangs
Plant Load
Sheppy Fen Hards
Mildenhall Drove & Drain
LAKENHEATH TOWN MO
MILDENHALL FEN
Prick Willow Bridge
L
A
Swag Corner
Mildenhall
Mow Fen
MILD
MILDENHALL COMMON FEN
H
U
West Row
THE
Isleham

Ferry House
LITTLE OUSE
BRANDON
Jo. Birch Esq.
77
Lakenheath
Mow Fen
Brandon Common Fen
Common to Lakenheath
Decoy
Lakenheath Swallard Fen
Lakenheath New Load
Cut-off Waters
76
Lakenheath Common Fen
Wangford Fen
Fish Pond
Grange
Sir Simeon Stuart
Wangford
TOWN MOOR
Lakenheath
75
Lakenheath Common
Water Load
Unley Fen
Elvedon Lodge
Unley Hards
C
K
74
F
O
Wangford Lodge
Eriswell Hall
Chapel in Ruins
Lakenheath Lodge
Baldwin's Load
Corner
Parsonage
73
Lower Lodge
MILDENHALL COMMON
High Lodge
72
Wild Street
FEN
Beck Row
Eriswell
Elvedon Gap
74
Holywell Row
Cake Street
71
73
U
N
D
R
E
72
West Row
Turnpike
Mildenhall Lodge
71
70
MILDENHALL
Barrows
Sir Cha. Bunbury
Barham
Seven Trees
Wamell Hall
Rushbrooke Esq.
70
RIVER
LARKE
Worlington
Barrows
Barrow
Ld. Chief Jus. De Grey
69
Little Barton
Stanch
Jn. Gwilt Esq.
68
Temple Br.
Icklingham St. James
TUDDENHAM FEN and HEATH
Icklingham All Saints
Freckenham
Rampit Close
Mill
67
Tuddenham
Lock
Cavenham Mill
Lackford Bridge
Lackford Green
66
Red Lodge
Hall
Lackford
Turnpike
Heringswell
2
Tho. Le Blanc Esq.
Cavenham

Downham
Ld. Cadogan
Santon
Stanch
Downham Lodge
Stanch
Brandon Lodge
Thetford Lodge
Lord Petre
Abbey
THETFORD
Cannons
St. Marys
79
Elvedon Lodge
R
D
Monastry
78
The Old London Road
77
Barnham Fen
Elvedon
76
Visc. Keppel
St. Martin
St. Gregory
Barnhams
Euston
75
74
Gap
9
Coach Way
Old Elvedon Gap
D
8
Wordwell Lodge
B
L
A
C
K
Fakenham
Rymer House
Barrows
Culford Lodge
Sheep Pin
LIVERMERE
HEATH
Barrows
Euston Ride
Seven Hills
Honington
6
New Farm
Rampit Close
Troston
H
U
N
Wordwell
Livermere Parva
5
Hall
Barham
Rushbrooke Esq.
West
Ampton
Livermere Magna
Bridge
Jas. Calthorpe Esq.
Stow
Lord Cornwallis
Culford
Lackford
Flempton
Ingham
Chimney Mill
Lackford Oaks
4
Timworth
Livermere
Pakenham
3

R
Rushford
Riddlesworth
Garboldisham
Gasthorpe
Gasthorpe Gate
Knattishall
Hopton Common
Hopton Gate
Blow Norton Hall
Revd. Mr. Browne
Fakenham Wood
Barningham Park
Cony Weston
Wm. Wollaston Esqr.
Barningham Heath
Hopton
Market Weston
Cross Green
Hedge Green
Weston Green
Fram. Thurston Esqr.
High Green
The Slade
Barningham
K
O
U
R
N
Playfords House
Bardwell Heath
Weston Pindle
Thelnetham Hall
Sand Pit House
Stanton Dale
Black Bridge
Sapiston
Hepworth
Bardwell Hall
Bardwell Green
Bardwell
St. John Stanton
All Saints
Hepworth Common
Watesfield Hall
Watesfield
High Wood
Stanton Hall
Thorp Green
Ixworth Thorp
D
Red House
Hall Green
Hell Green
Westhall Wood
Upthorp Common
Wyken Hall
Walsham
IXWORTH
Wood Street
Langham Thicks
Langham Comn.
Crowland
Brick Kiln
Sir Pat. Blake
Badwell Green
Badwell Ash
Hall
Badwell Thicks
Pakenham Hall
Langham
Tiptod
Pakenham Fen
Stowlangtoft
Hunston
Arthur Heigham Esqr.
Ashfield
Pakenham Common
Beaumond Hall
Hunston Hall
Brazier Lane
Days Green
Barton Mere
Nether Hall
Pakenham
Norton Moor
Norton
A
S
I
R
E
Ashfield Haugh
Boten Haugh Green
Ashfield Lee
Thurston
Thurston Green
Norton Hall
High Street
Bacton Hall
Crawley Hall
Thurston Heath
Elmswell Hall
Wetherden Hall
4

Lopham

F O

Brisingham

DISS

Fen Street

Lopham Ford Gate

Fen

Common

Rev.d Mr. Betts

Wortham Hall

Redgrave

Magpye Green

Wortham

Palgrave

Rev.d Mr. Palgrave

Mr. Barker

Rev.d Mr. Graves

Redgrave Green

Wortham Green

Stuston Com.

Old Hall

Stuston

Hinderclay Hall

Rowland Holt Esq.r

Wortham Marsh

18

19

20

21

Thrandiston Marsh

Thrandiston Great Green

Little Green

Broom Hill

North Mill

16

17

Burgate

Brook

Burgate Great Green

Thrandiston

Parsonage

Snape Green

Rickinghall Inferior

BOTESDALE

14

Burgate Hall

Gosland Hall

Broome Common

Earl

Burgate Little Green

Parsonage

Sugland Gr.

Botesdale Green

Reydon Slough

Rickinghall Superior

Mellis Hall

T. Clarke Esq.r

Mellis Green

Yaxley

23

Bacons Hall

H A R T I S M E R

Yaxley Hall

Moor Hall

Park Way

Thornham Parva

124

Alnood Green

Gislingham

Parsonage

Swatsal Hall

Great Thornham Hall

Red House

Dow.r Dutc.s of Chandos

Thornham Magna

Park

Rush Green

25

Gull Slaugh

Westhorp Lodge

Star House

Braisworth

Braisworth Hall

Finningham Hall

Dog House

Stoke Ash

Wood Hall

Combe Hall

Nutmeg Green

Hall

Finningham

Westhorp

Green

Birds Hedge

26

Stoke Bowling Green

Thorndon Green

Wyverston Park

Wickham Abby

Wickham Skeith

Thorndon

Green

Wickham Hills

Mill-gate Way

H U N D R E D

Wyverston Parsonage

Thwaite

Park

Hemnens Hall

Thwaite Hall

27

Rishangle

Alice Gr.

Bacton

Green

Cotton

Brockford

Rishangles Lodge

Shorts

Hazely Hall

Parsonage

Pest House

Hall Brockford

Street

Brames Hall

Bacton Green

Parsonage

Carters Green

Wetheringset

Hazely Gr.

Topper Hill

28

Smiths Green

Cotton Hall

MENDLESHAM

Wetheringset Hall

Knaves Gr.

Parsonage

Wetheringset Lodge

Wetheringset Green

5

Old Bells

Whitaps Knowl

Worswicks

Brockford

Great

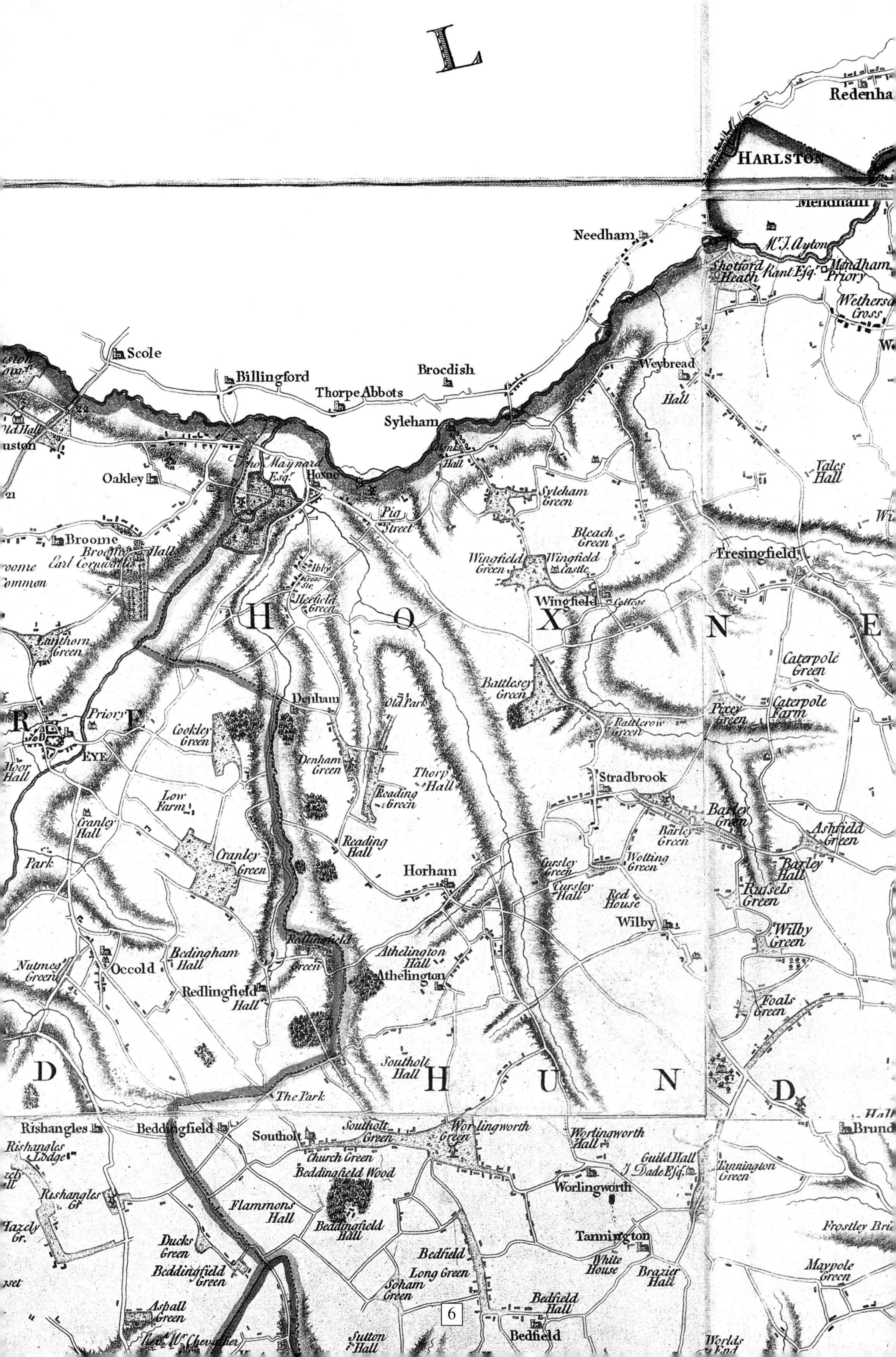
L
Redenha
HARLSTON
Mendham
Needham
Mr. J. Ayton
Shotford Heath
Kant Esq.
Mendham Priory
Wethersa Cross
Scole
Billingford
Brocdish
Thorpe Abbots
Syleham
Weybread Hall
Oakley
Hoxne
Thos. Maynard Esq.
Monks Hall
Syleham Green
Vales Hall
Pig Street
Bleach Green
Broome
Broome Hall
Earl Cornwallis
Broome Common
Wingfield Green
Wingfield Castle
Fresingfield
Abby
Cross Str.
Heefield Green
Wingfield
College
Lanthorn Green
H O X N E
Caterpole Green
Battlesey Green
Denham
Old Park
Caterpole Farm
Pixey Green
Battlerow Green
Priory
EYE
Cookley Green
Denham Green
Moor Hall
Thorp Hall
Stradbrook
Reading Green
Low Farm
Barley Green
Cranley Hall
Ashfield Green
Reading Hall
Barley Green
Park
Cranley Green
Cursley Green
Wolting Green
Horham
Barley Hall
Cursley Hall
Red House
Russels Green
Wilby
Wilby Green
Redlingfield Green
Athelington Hall
Nutmeg Green
Bedingham Hall
Occold
Athelington
Foals Green
Redlingfield Hall
Southolt Hall
D
H U N D
The Park
Rishangles
Beddingfield
Southolt
Southolt Green
Worlingworth Green
Worlingworth Hall
Brund
Rishangles Lodge
Church Green
Guild Hall
J. Dade Esq.
Tannington Green
Beddingfield Wood
Worlingworth
Rishangles Gr.
Flammons Hall
Frostley Bri
Hazely Gr.
Beddingfield Hall
Tannington
Ducks Green
Bedfield
Beddingfield Green
White House
Brazier Hall
Maypole Green
Long Green
Soham Green
Bedfield Hall
Aspall Green
Bedfield
Sutton Hall
Worlds End

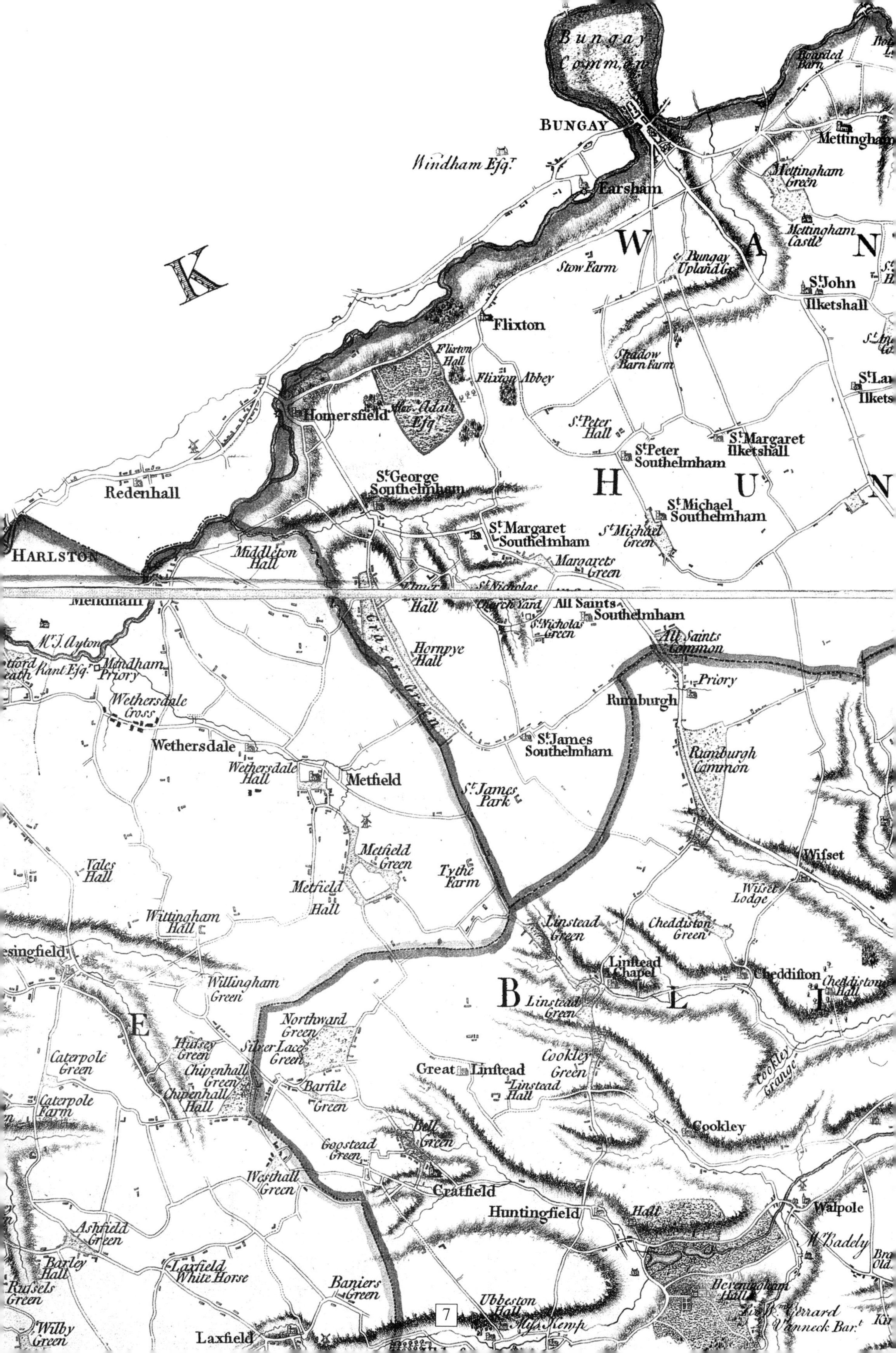

Bungay Common
BUNGAY
Windham Esqr.
Earsham
Mettingham
Mettingham Green
Mettingham Castle
K
W
A
N
Stow Farm
Bungay Upland Gr.
St. John Ilketshall
Flixton
Flixton Hall
Flixton Abbey
Shaddow Barn Farm
Homersfield
Alexr. Adair Esqr.
St. Peter Hall
St. Peter Southelmham
St. Margaret Ilketshall
Redenhall
St. George Southelmham
H
U
N
St. Michael Southelmham
St. Michael Green
St. Margaret Southelmham
HARLSTON
Middleton Hall
Margarets Green
Mendham
Hall
Church Yard
All Saints Southelmham
St. Nicholas Green
Mr. J. Ayton
Hornpye Hall
All Saints Common
Kant Esqr.
Mendham Priory
Wethersdale Cross
Priory
Rumburgh
Wethersdale
St. James Southelmham
Wethersdale Hall
Metfield
Rumburgh Common
St. James Park
Metfield Green
Wisset
Vales Hall
Tythe Farm
Metfield Hall
Wisset Lodge
Wittingham Hall
Linstead Green
Cheddiston Green
Linstead Chapel
Cheddiston
Cheddiston Hall
Willingham Green
B
Linstead Green
L
E
Northward Green
Hulsey Green
Silver Laces Green
Cookley Green
Caterpole Green
Chipenhall Green
Great Linstead
Cookley Grange
Barfile Green
Linstead Hall
Chipenhall Hall
Caterpole Farm
Cookley
Bell Green
Goostead Green
Westhall Green
Cratfield
Huntingfield
Hall
Walpole
Ashfield Green
Mr. Badely
Barley Hall
Laxfield White Horse
Heveningham Hall
Rufsels Green
Baniers Green
Ubbeston Hall
Sir Gerrard Vanneck Bart.
Mrs. Kemp
Wilby Green
Laxfield

London Road
St. Matthews Street
George Lane
Clay Lane
Hill Lane
St. Matthews
Church Lane
Lady Lane
Westgate Street
to Hanford Bridge
Tan Yard
Hanford Mill
Corn Hill
Town H.
Tavern Street
St. Mary Tower
St. Mary Elms
Burial or Coal Lane
St. Laurence
Butter Market
St. Stephens
Portmans Walks
Friers
Br.
Boat Lane
Falcon Lane
Queen Street
Nicholas Str.
Grey Friers Road
Brook Street
St. Peters
College
Bridge
Stoke Mill
St. Mary Stoke
Pound
Work House

PLAN
OF THE
TOWN
OF
IPSWICH.
Scale of Yards.
Christs Ch
Bowling Green
St Margarets
Bolton Lane
Soane Street
Margarets Ditches
St Margarets
Road to Woodbridge
St Helens Wash
St Helens
Rope Lane
Gram School
Christ H.
Shire Hall
St Clements
Church Lane
St Clements
New Street
Key Street
Custom H.
Fore Street
Wykes
Hamlet
RIVER
ORWELL
Ship Yards

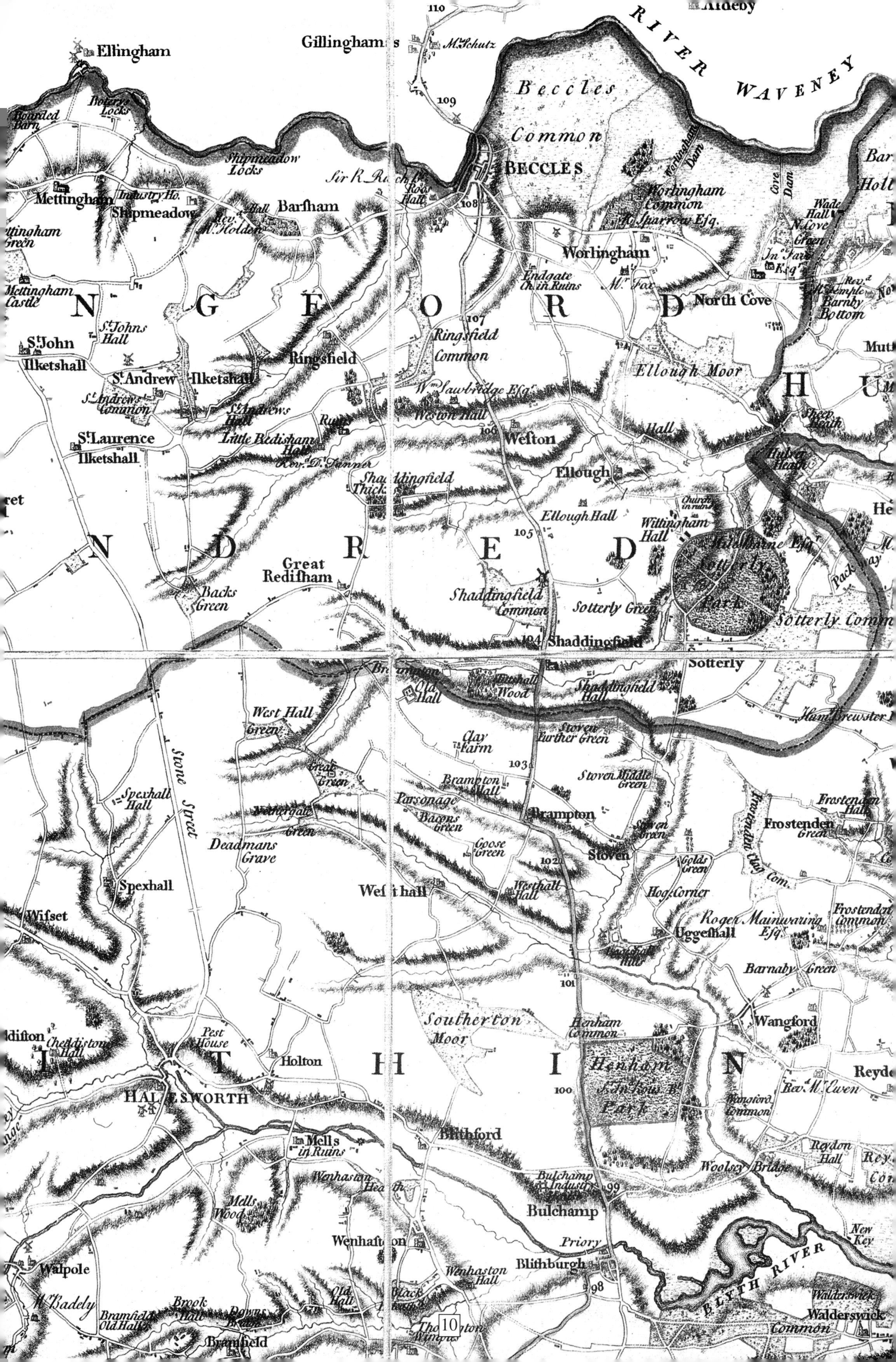

110
Aldeby
RIVER WAVENEY
Ellingham
Gillingham
Mr. Schutz
Beccles Common
109
Boarded Barn
Botterys Locks
Shipmeadow Locks
Sir R. Rich
Ross Hall
BECCLES
Worlingham Dam
Cove Dam
Bar
Holt
Mettingham
Industry Ho.
Shipmeadow
Hall
Rev. Mr. Holden
Barsham
108
Worlingham Common
R. Sparrow Esq.
Wade Hall
N. Cove Green
Mettingham Green
Worlingham
Jn. Farr Esq.
Endgate Ch. in Ruins
Mr. Fox
Rev. Temple
Mettingham Castle
N G F O R D
North Cove
Barnby Bottom
107
St. Johns Hall
St. John Ilketshall
Ringsfield Common
Ringsfield
Ellough Moor
Mutt
St. Andrew Ilketshall
St. Andrews Common
Wm. Sawbridge Esq.
H U
Weston Hall
St. Andrews Hall
Sheep Heath
Ruin
Hall
106
St. Laurence Ilketshall
Little Redisham Hall
Weston
Rev. Dr. Tanner
Ellough
Hulver Heath
Shaddingfield Thicks
Church in ruins
He
Ellough Hall
Willingham Hall
105
Miles Barne Esq.
N D R E D
Great Redisham
Sotterly Park
Pack way
Backs Green
Shaddingfield Common
Sotterly Green
Sotterly Common
104
Shaddingfield
Brampton
Old Hall
Sotterly
Ritshall Wood
Shaddingfield Hall
Ham Brewster
West Hall Green
Stoven Further Green
Clay Farm
103
Great Green
Stoven Middle Green
Stone Street
Spexhall Hall
Brampton Hall
Frostenden Hall
Parsonage
Frostenden Green
Wetheringate Green
Bacons Green
Brampton
Frostenden Clay Com.
Deadmans Grave
Goose Green
Stoven Green
Stoven
102
Golds Green
Spexhall
Westhall
Westhall Hall
Hog Corner
Wisset
Roger Mainwaring Esq.
Frostenden Common
Uggeshall
Barnaby Green
101
Wangford
Southerton Moor
Henham Common
Pest House
Chediston Hall
Holton
T H I N
Reyd
Henham Sir Jn. Rous B. Park
Rev. Mr. Ewen
100
HALESWORTH
Wangford Common
Blithford
Mells in Ruins
Reydon Hall
Woolsey Bridge
Wenhaston Heath
Bulchamp Industry
99
Mells Wood
Bulchamp
New Key
Wenhaston
Priory
BLYTH RIVER
Walpole
Blithburgh
Wenhaston Hall
Walderswick
Mr. Badely
Old Hall
98
Brook Hall
Black Heath
Bramfield Old Hall
Downs Farm
Walderswick Common
Bramfield
Thorington

GREAT YARMOUTH
BREYDON WATER
West Town
South Town
Bradwell Common
Burgh Common
Gorleston Fen
Burgh Castle
Gorleston
Hall
Bradwell
Belton Common
FORT
Belton
LOTHINGLAND
Belton Hall
Broceston Hall
Hobland Hall
Gorleston Common
Dr. Urquhart Esq.
Caldecot Hall
Fritton Common
Hopton Com.
Fritton
Ashbye Warren
Lound Common
St. Olaves Priory
St. Olaves Bridge
Heringfleet Common
Blocker Hall Leake Esq.
Lound Green
Hopton
Lound
Ashbye
West Heath
Heringfleet
Blundeston
Somerliton Hall
Hadsco Dam
Hadsco
Corton
Manthorp Gr.
Sir Thos. Allen Bar.t
Somerliton
Blundeston
Miss Allen
Blundeston Hall
HUNDRED
Corton Heath
Flixton
Industry House
Flixton Common
Gunton
Hall
Dr. Saunders
High House
Thos. Anguish Esq.
Oulton Common
Whitacre
Burrough
Aldeby
Oulton
Light House
Light House
Normanston
LOWESTOFT
RIVER WAVENEY
LAKE LOTHING
Oulton Dike
Carlton
Carlton Shares
Kirkley Heath
Barnby
Holbourn
Burnt Hill
Whitton Green
Kirkley
Worlingham Common
Sparrow Esq.
Wade Hall
MUTFORD
Pakefield
Barnby Common
Carlton Colvile
Hall
Carlton Green
11

North Cove
Barnby Bottom
Muthall Common
Mutford
Gisleham
Ellough Moor
H U N D R E D
Mutford Com.
Rushmere
Rusthill Heath
Sheep Heath
Hall
Hulsey Heath
Rushmere Hall
Rushmere Bridge
Mr. Clark
Henstead
Snubs Bottom
Barton Com.
Kessingland Common
Kessingland
Wittingham Hall
Henstead Green
Sotterly Park
Pack way
Savage Wood
Sotterly Common
Sotterly
Sir Tho. Gooch
Wrentham Hall
Park
Sluice
Wrentham
Pye Hall
Frostenden Hall
Frostenden
Frostenden Green
Wrentham Common
Covehith Common
Covehith
Golds Green
Hog Corner
Roger Mainwaring Esq.
Frostenden common
South Cove
Uggeshall
Barnaby Green
Cove Common
Wangford
Easton Broad
Potters Bridge
N
Reydon
Rev. Mr. Ewen
Easton Bavent
Wangford Common
Park
Reydon Hall
Reydon Common
Woolsey Bridge
Southwould Bridge
Old Key
New Key
BLYTH RIVER
SOUTHWOULD
Black Shore
Walderswick
Walderswick Common
T H E
Westwood Lodge
Great Dingley
DUNWICH RIVER
Little Dingley
D
DUNWICH

Isleham
Freckenham
Hall
Exning Common
Lanwade
Snailwell
Part of
Exning
Burwell
Lackford
Hundred
NEWMARKET
Kings Chair
Hawk Ladder
Moul
DEVILS
DYKE
Running Gap
Dukes Course
Kings Gap
Well Gap
Cambridge Gap
Round Course
Turnpike
59
60
61
63
63
64
65

Red Lodge
Turnpike
Heringswell
Lackford Green
Lackford
Cavenham
Tho.s Le Blanc Esq.
Turnpike
Kennet
Diney Lodge
Kentford
Carmerow Bridge
Higham Lower Green
Needham Street
Broom Wood
Saxham White Horse
T
H
I
Moulton
Moulton Hall
Middle Green
Upper Green
Parsonage
Barrow
Burthorp Green
Heath End
Gazely
Great Saxham
Disnage Hall
Barrow Green
Denham End
Denham Castle
Carwick Bridge
Gill Affleck Esq.r
Dalham
Denham Hall
Tunstall Green
Hargrave
Chevington Lodge
Chevington
Oueſden
Ousden Hall
Wil. Moseley Esq.r
South Park
Cropley Park
H
U
N
Castle
Lidgate
Baxters Green
Genesis Green
Badmondesfield Hall
Nath. Barret
Depden Hall
Depden
Chedburgh
Aldersfield Hall
Depden Elms
Reed Green
Fr. Dickins Esq.
Branches Hall
Moor Green
Coltswot Green
Gipsas End
Cooling Frith
Cooling
Gains Hall
Aulton Green
Dods
Gainsbury's
Wickham Brook
Fairstead
Oaks
Clapton Green
R
I
S
B
R
I
D
G
E
East Green
Lamb Fair
Pound Green
Cardwell Hole
Giffords
Farley Green
Hobbles Green
Pulten Hall
Pulten Green
Wickham House
Denston
Stradishall
Hawkedon
Sheep Cut
Stansfield
Three Ashes
Bradley
Nices Denston
Thurstaston
14

Lackford
Elempton
Stow
Chimney Mill
Culford
Ingham
Timworth
Livermere
Thicks
Pakenham Heath
Red Castle
Lackford Oaks
Fornham St. Genoveve
Sir Cha. Kent
Hengrave
Warren Hill Pin
Stanch Farm
Fornham All Saints
Wm. Moseley Esq.
Rev. John Ord
Fornham St. Martin
Hide
Conyard Green
H. Bunbury Esq.
Sir Cha. Bunbury
Risby
Wharf
Friery
Mer Maid Pitts
THEDWA
Barton
Catshall Green
NGOE
Turnpike
Heath End
Covey Wood
Westley
BURY
ST. EDMUNDS
St. Edmunds Hill
John Symonds Esq.
Elder House
Little Saxham
Little Saxham Hall
R. Crokes Esq.
Woodland
Horringer Hall
Horningsherth
Hardwick House
Rev. Sir John Cullum Bart.
Horse Croft
Rushbrook
Rougham Green
Ickworth
Horringer Green
Low Green
Hall
Sir Cha. Davers
Kingshall Green
Earl of Bristol
Nowton Hall
Hawstead Lodge
Hawstead Place
Bradfield Green
Bradfield
St. George
Welnetham Parva
NDRED
Smiths Green
Pinford End Hall
Hawstead
Welnetham Mag.
Copdocks Hall
HU
Raw Hall
Hall Bush Green
Duffen Hall
Broad Gate
Chaple House
Raw Hall Wood
Elding Wood
Hay Green
Hawstead Farm
Whepstead
Plumpton
Reed Hall
Hall
Mickley Green
Stone Cross Green
Moor Green
A. Young Esq.
Chedburgh
Melon Green
Bradfield Combust
Bradfield St. Clare
Reed Kiln
Stanningfield
Stanningfield Green
Bradfield Bush
Old Hall Green
Gurland Green
Menston Hall
Reed
Reed Green
Talmage
Shepherds Nap
Round Green
Cages Green
Coldham Hall
Little Saxs
Loft Farm
Seymers
Pepper
Broad Green
Hall
Brockley
Pickards
Harts Green
Great Saxs Farm
Cockfield
Herberts Green
Windsor Green
Parsonage Green
Gipsies End
Brockley Green
Whitage
Darney
Hall
Hinyfields Green
E
Longs
Lawshall
Langley
Walgrave
Haws
Burnt House
Lawshall Green
Earls Hall
Cooks
Shimpling Street
Rev. Mr. Fiske
Somerton
Hartest
Chadacre Hall
Hole Farm
Hall Barn
Mile End
Harteft
Shimpling Park
15

Thurston
Norton Hall
Heath
Green
High Street
Bacton Hall
Rev. Mr. Tyrell
Crawley Hall
Thurston Heath
Elmswell Hall
Darshams
Wetherden Hall
Hawleigh Green
Tyson Esq.
Tostock
Elmswell
Rook Yard
Rougham
Beighton
Little London
Wetherden
Beighton Brook
Woolpit
Richd. Ray Esq.
Hawleigh Castle
Rougham High Street
Hessett
Hessett Hall
Rev. Mr. Moseley
Hawleigh Park
Edw. Sulyard Esq.
Drinkston
Woolpit Heath
Woolpit Green
Woolpit & Shelland Woods
Squares Cross
Fish Pond Green
Mr. Leheup Esq.
Hicket
Heath
Bushes House
Sheepcote Green
Marsh Green
Rockylls Hall
Shelland Gr.
Tot Hill
Drinkston Green
Clopton Green
Harleston Green
Harleston
Hall
St. George
Drinkston Hall
Clopton Hall
Shelland Hall
Shelland
N D R E D
Tanning Office Farm
May Pole Green
Smallwood Green
Rattlesden
Onehouse
Hedge Wood
Gedding Hall
Fen Street
Hall
Pitchers Green
Gedding
Poy Street Green
St. Clare Hall
How Wood
Wm. Pollaston Esq.
Bradfield St. Clare
Felsham Abbey Wood
Monks Park
Buxhall
Boyton Hall
Hall
Felsham
Hightown Green
Great Finborough
Fosborns Hall
H U N D
Broad Green
Thorp Wood
Oxes Green
Rattlesden Wood
Hoistead Green
Keely Grove
Brastead Green
Colchester Green
Parsonage Green
Bull Wood
Thorpe Green
Hasting Wood
Pye Hatch
Little Finborough
Brettenham
Hitcham Wood
East Wood
B
Thorpe Morieux
Parsonage
Buttons Green
Hall
Charles Hall
Parsonage Wood
Brettenham Hall
J. Menyere Esq.
Cross Green
Deer Wood
Parsonage Hall
Charles Tye
Beeson Grove
Bircham Grove
Dead Mans Wood
Wattisham
New House
H
C O S F O R D
Hall
Hitcham
Green
Scapes Grove
Priory
Bricet
Preston
Kettlebarston
Green Street Green
LAVENHAM
BILDESTON
Nedging Tye
Naughton Hall
Brent Eleigh Tye
Naughton
Edw. Goate Esq.
Chelsworth
Brent Eleigh
Parsonage
Nedging Hall
Cutts Wood
Monks Illeigh
Robt. Pocklington Esq.
Washmore Green
Bret River
Wells Hall
Whatfield Hall
Semer

MENDLESHAM
Parsonage
Whiteups Knowl
Smiths Green
Cotton Hall
Old Bells
Worsracks
New Bells
Gipping
Rook Yard House
Cross Green
Newton
Otertons Green
Fish Pond Bridge
Dagworth Hall
Gipping Wood
Cay Hill
Mendlesham Green
Tanning Office
Knaves Gr.
Wetheringset Hall
Wetheringset Lodge
Wetheringset Green
Brockford Green
Great Green
Westrup Street
Old Hall
Rumble Green
Waltham Hall
Mickfield Hall
Gosling Hall
Saxham Street
Middlewood Green
Mickfield
Columbine Hall
Thorney Green
Dear Wood
Clock House Farm
Stonham Parva
Stonham Pye
Parsonage
Tidymans Green
Forward Green
Northern Green
Old Mewness
Dagger House
Spulmans House
Thorney Hall
STOW MARKET
Sheep Gate Hall
Broad Green
Raydon Hall
Earl Stonham
Parsonage
Stonham Aspall
Broughton Hall
Old East End
Turnpike
Greeting Green
Creeting Hall
West Creeting
Dear Bought Hall
Stonham Green
Creeting Bottom
Crowfield
Crowfield Green
Woolney Hall
Creeting St. Olives in Ruins
Burnt Mill
Combs Hill
Trickers Hill
Creeting Hall
All Saints
Creeting St. Mary
Jacks Green
Wm. Middleton Esq.
Crowfield Hall
Greeting College
Hall
Badley
Badley Green
Moats Tye
Dods
Paper Hill
Holts
NEEDHAM
Battisford
Coppings Hall
Gofbeck
Battisford St. Johns
Hosmere Bush
Hungry Gut Hall
Bridge Place
Vicarage
Saml. Uvedale Esq.
Bacon Hill
Codenham
Stone Wall
Hascot Hill
Barking
Chas. Hoone Esq.
Hall
Ringshall
Hall
Pips
Darmsden
Eiver Mere
Pool House
Olivers Green
Hall
Hemingstone
Tower
Shrubland Hall
Revd. Nich. Bacon
John Bacon Esq.
Barking Tye
Ringshall Green
Taston Hall
Baylham Hall
Baylham
Baylham Str.
Bells Cross
Willisham Green
Sharpston
Street
Barham Green
Willisham Hall
Willisham
Newmans Green
Blakenham Magna
Work House
Barham
Henley
Hall
Tallemach Hall
High Hall
Turnpike
Hackneys Corner
Wm. Medows Theobald Esq.
Rougham Hall
Henly Reed
Hall
Ofton
Nettlestead
Green
Hall
Turnpike
Claydon
Revd. Mr. Drury
Parsonage
Ofton Castle
Akenham Hall
Blakenham Parva
Blakenham Common
Claydon Hall
Kelly Green
Somersham
Mock Beggars Hall
Rice Hall
Hall
Sicamore
Thurlston
T O W
R E D
O S M E R E
A N D
C L A Y
I L N D R E D
28
29
30
31
32
33
34
35
36
37
38
39
12
13
14
15
16
17
18
19
20
21
22

Tannington
Ducks Green
Beddingfield Green
Bedfield
Long Green
Soham Green
White House
Brazier Hall
Maypole Green
Aspall Green
Bedfield Hall
Bedfield
Sutton Hall
Kenton
Aspall
Hunger Green
Worlds End
Saxstead
Saxstead Stulps
Kenton Hall
White House
Soham Hall
Monk Soham
Little Bedfield Green
Rumble Green
DEBENHAM
Woodcroft Hall
Saxstead Green
Tuttons Corner
Clough Corner
Soham Lodge
Gosting Hall
Camps Green
Crows Hall
Ashfield Hall
Earl Soham
Ashfield
Ruins
White Hall
Thorp
Apsey Green
THREDLING
Winston
Winston Green
Lamford Brook
L O E
HUNDRED
Old East End
Pettaugh
Cretingham
Bramdeston
Kettleborough Common
Kettleborough
Framsden
Lewis House
Kettleborough Green
Pettaugh Hall
Abbots Hall
Bocking Hall
Monewden Hall
R. Sparrow Esq.
Monewden Folly
Monewden Green
Monewden
Hoo Green
Hoo
Letheringham
Priory
Helmingham
Earl of Dysart
Monewden Red House
Hoo Spring
Charsfield Spring
Gosbeck Green
Barnes Wood
Monewden Post
H U N D
Letheringham Lodge
Otley Wood
Otley Hall
Otley Green
Charsfield
Gosbeck
Y D O N
Ash Hall
Ashbocken
Otley
Parsonage
Clapton Green
Ash Green
Otley Bottom
Dallinghoo Wood
Dallinghoe
Debach
Cats Hills
Brand Hall
Pot Ash
Henley Broad Green
Hall
Swilland
Hopwell Green
Bredfield Green
Henley Green
Thistleton Hall
Bredfield
Ufford Thicks
Clopton
Parsonage
Burgh
Bouldge
Knoppit Knowl
Winyland
Sky Green
Sycamore
Rigs Hill
Witnesham
Wood
Grundisburgh
Hewits Spring
Melton Indus. House
Squerels Grove
Hasketon
Hall
CARLFORD
Part of Loes Hundred
Farthing Cake Hall
WOODBRIDGE
B. G. Dillingham Esq.
Culpho
Hall
Culpho Hall
Great Bealings
18
77
78

Laxfield
Ubbeston
Heveningham
Ubbeston Green
Foals Green
Boats Hall
Parkfield
Sibton Green
Little Green
Owl Green
D R E D
H U
Brundish
Baddingham Hall
Bowling Green
Peasenhall
Sibton Abby
Sibton
Pennington Hall
Frostley Bridge
Baddingham
Badingham Green
Maypole Green
Cape Green
Apcot Bridge
Rooks Bridge
Sibton Grange
Dennington
White H
Colston Hall
Rotten End
Saxstead Stulps
Bruisyard
Bruisyard Hall
Great Lodge
Countess's Well
Little Lodge
Rendham Green
Cransford Green
Cransford
Bubling Green
Part
Hams Green
Callow Gr.
Carlton Green
Hoxne
Castle
Rendham
Swefling
FRAMLINGHAM
Kilderbees Grove
Osborn Fuller Esq.
Carlton
Apsey Green
Coles Green
Cold Hall
Dernford Hall
Dods Wood
Parham House
Northern Green
Lamford Brook
E
S
Mill Farm
Sam Rush Esq.
Benhall
North Glemham
Benhall Lodge
Kettleborough Green
Cutlers Green
Silver lace Green
Parham
Benhall Street
Kelton End
Free School
Benhall Green
Stock Ho.
Hickland Hall
Parham Hall
Marlesford Green
Wood Farm
Stratford St Andrews
Farnham
Farnham Hall
Earl of Rochford
Blomville Hall
Easton
Hacheston
Marlesford
Whimpers Wood
Glemham Parva
Priory
Letheringham Hall
Pistree Hall
Rock Yard
Bedens Grove
N D R E D
P I O M
Burnt House
Langham Bridge
Snape Abby
Letheringham Lodge
Beversham Brigg
Water Common
Parsonage
Blaxhall Hall
Glevering Hall
Snape
Potchards Hills
Blackstock Watering
Blaxhall Common
Wickham Market
Campsey Ash
Rotten Row
Kiln Ground
White Cross La.
Pettistree
Ash Com.
Ash Park Farm
Tunstall
Heath
Campsey Mere
Ash Green
Moat Ho.
Campsey Abby
Hamilton
Rendesham White Ho.
Sandpit Ho.
Hopwell Green
Ufford
Bredfield
19

Mells in Ruins
Wenhaston Heath
Mells Wood
Wenhaston
Walpole
Bulchamp
Priory
Blithburgh
BLYTH RIVER
Walderswick
Walderswick Common
Woolsey Bridge
Reydon Hall
New Key
Bramfield Old Hall
Brook Hall
Bramfield
Bramfield Hall
Kingsale Wood
Thorington
Thorington Wimples
Wenhaston Hall
Westwood Lodge
Halls way
Hinton High Ash
Thorington Hall
G. Golding Esq.
Thorington Common
Hinton Hall
Great Dingley
Little Dingley
DUNWICH RIVER
Sibton Green
Little Green
Sibton Great Green
Hinton
N
D
R
D
Yoxford Wood
Brick Kiln
DUNWICH
Darsham
Cockfield Hall
Hog Hill
Yoxford
Westleton
Westleton Common
Middleton
Middleton Moor
Rackway Bridge
Fordley
Scotts Hall
Sluice House
Minsmer Haven
The Broad
Yewtree Hou.
Theberton
East Bridge Street
Common Fen
Old Chapel
North Green
of
Kelsale Manor House
East Green
Callow Gr.
Carlton Green
Hundred
White Cross
Carlton
Maple House
Buxlow
Forest
Potters Street
Old Lady Abby Farm
Leiston Abby
Tylers Green
Wet Common
Dry Common
SAXMUNDHAM
Knoddishall Green
Leiston
Hall
Great House
Knoddishall Hall
Sternfield
Friston Moor
Coldford Green
Aldringham Common
Thorp Common
Buxlow
Friston Hall
Friston
Bulls Hall
Bilsey Hall
Aldringham
Thorpe Ruins
Thelford Watering
Snape
Friston Green
Park Farm
O
M
E
S
G
A
T
E
G
Rook Yard
Friston Decoy
Haslewood in Ruins
Snape Abby
Langham Bridge
Snape Bridge
Warren Ho.
20

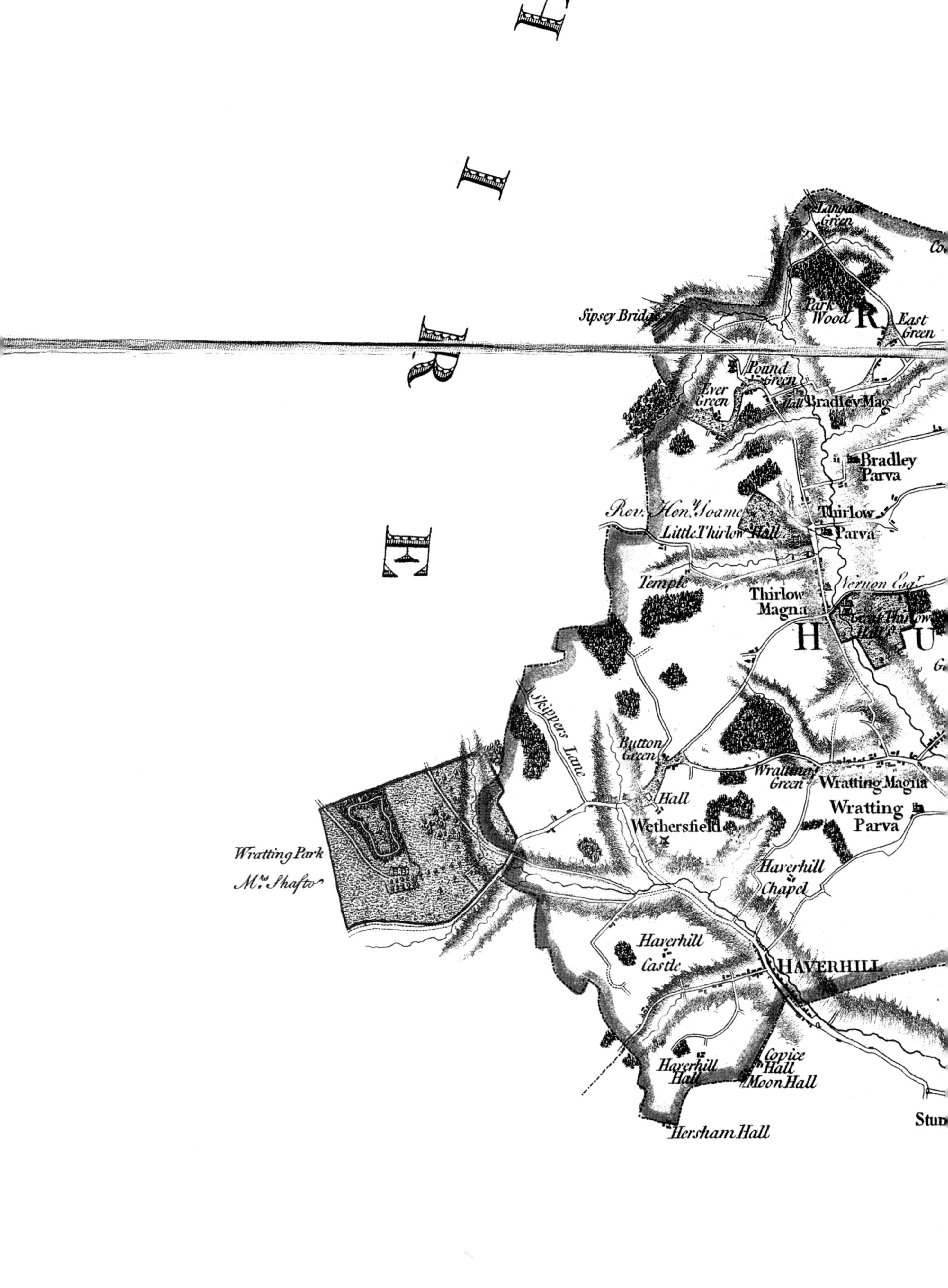

Sipsey Bridg
Park Wood
East Green
Pound Green
Ever Green
Bradley Mag
Bradley Parva
Rev. Hen. Soame
Little Thirlow Hall
Thirlow Parva
Temple
Thirlow Magna
Vernon Esq.
Skippers Lane
Button Green
Wratting Green
Wratting Magna
Hall
Wratting Parva
Wethersfield
Wratting Park
Mrs. Shafto
Haverhill Chapel
Haverhill Castle
HAVERHILL
Copice Hall
Haverhill Hall
Moon Hall
Hersham Hall

Lidgate
Baxters Green
Genesis Green
Badmondesfield Hall
Nath Barret Esq.
Depden Hall
Depden
Chedburgh
Reed Kiln
Reed
Reed Green
Depden Elms
Gipses End
Gainsburys
Fr. Dickins Esq.
Branches Hall
Cooling Frith
Cooling
Fairstead
Lamb Fair
Pound Green
East Green
Oaks
Attilton Green
Gains Hall
Moor Green
Coltswort Green
Aldersfield Hall
Dods
Wickham Brook
Clapton Green
Cardwell Hole
Giffords
Farley Green
Hobbles Green
Bradley Parva
Three Ashes
Stradishall
Denston
Wickham House
Putten Hall
Putten Green
Sheep Cut
Hawkedon
Stansfield
Thurstruston Hall
Nices
Denston Hall
Mashes
John Robinson Esq.r
Hill Farm
Great Lodge
Halaky
Broxley Lodge
Monks Farm
Barnardiston Hall
Great Thurlow Hall
Aston End Green
Baymans
Elm Farm
Thurstruston End
Stansfield Hall
Swan Hall
Eastry Lodge
Gosland Green
Shadow Bush
Chipley Abbey
Garwick
Hundon Hall
Hundon
Hundon Thicks
Tinverton
Barnardiston
Chimney Street
Babbel Green
Highfields
Pynner Hall
Clock Hall
Kedington Leys
Wratting Magna
Wratting Parva
Brackhall Green
Hall
Kedington
Dye Syer D.D.
Way Bank
Arkum Street
Folley
Poslingford
Wow Hall
Wales End
Cavendish Lodge
Robs Farm
Colts Hall
Ark Farm
Chilton Street
Chilton Hall
Wentford House
Holton Hall
Hermitage
Chilton Chapel
Hill Farm
Cotton Hall
CLARE
Castle
Clare Mill
Priory
Padd Bow Hall
Sturmer Mere
Sturmer
Water Hall
Wixoe
Moor Hall
Ashen Mill
Stoke
H. Elwes
Stoke College
Stoke Mill
Baythorn End
Baythorn Pa
Ashen or Esse
Ovington
Belchamp St. Paul
S U R I D G E
U N D R E D
E

Swan Hall
Moat Fart
Moors
Giffords
Deals
Shimpling
Elm Farm
64
B
A
B
E
R
G
Title Hall
Boxted Hall
Bulls Hall
Hall
Alpheaton Tye
Clap Stile
Boxted
Spring Hall
Coppings Farm
Alpheton
Park Farm
Rudsrow
Bragens
Roughedge
Farnel
Jankens
Plumb Street
Stanstead
Dunton
Brights
Moors
Leys
New Street
John Moore Esq.
Ford Hall
Glemsford
Barston Hall
Robs Farm
Colts Hall
Court Farm
Spilton Wood
Grammoor Green
Thumbs
Vicarage
Town Farm
Blackland
Washmore Green
Cavendish
Buttons
Lodge Farm
Cavendish Place
Weston Mill
Beards
Brandeston Hall
Pentlow
Melford Hall
Paddock Mill
Bower Hall
Paper Mill
59
Long Melford
Acton Hall
Sir Edm.d Bacon
Acton
Wood Hall
Holbrook Hall
Liston
Foxearth
H
N
D
Whittingham Mill
Stalage
Newmans Green
Babergh Heath
Cox Green
Tye
St. Paul
Rodbridge
Waldingfield
Magna
Wood Hall
Boreley
St. Bartholomew
58
Morris
Badleys
Mill
Chilton Hall
Edwardstone Park
Brunden Mill & Hall
57
Chilton
Cornard Heath
SUDBURY
Butlers
Ballingdon
Newton
Cornard Mag
Broom Street
Abbot Hall
Deans Brooks
Mill Tye
Wrongs
Little Grais
Great Grais
From London
Black House
Cornard Parva
Park Farm
S
Parsonage
Giblands
Kersons
Great Henny
Sawyers
Darking Tye
Lammarsh
Bures

Washmore Green
Wells Hall
River
Semer
Whatfield Hall
Brandeston Hall
Nether Hall
Milding
Milding Hall
Hall
Rev. Mr. Cooke
Ash Street
Furnace
Whatfield
Wood Hall
Humble Green
Slackyard Green
Milding Pound
Ravens Hall
Lindsey Tye
Greetston Green
Ballad Hall
Waldingfield Parva
Milding Green
Lindsey
Semer Industry House
H U N D R E
R E D
Hall
Rose Green
Chapel
Strangers Green
Kersey Priory
Kersey
Edwardston Priory
Nokes Tye
Stone Street
Brook Street
Grove
Parliament Heath
Kersey Tye
Sir Tho. Thorowgood
Sampsons Hall
Hadleigh Place
HADLEIGH
Badleys
Whistlers Green
Broad Street
Castling Heath
Leaves Green
Kersey Hole
Edwardston Park
Mill Green
S. Leeke
Quoits Gr.
Withermarsh Green
Hall
Edwardston
Boar House
Wicker Street Green
Hobbets
Rev. A. H. Newcomb
Walnuttree House
Hall
Butlers
Shaver Street
Grotton
Evans Heath
Hadleigh Heath
8
Benton End
Newton
Deans Brooks
Boxford
Mock Beggar Green
63
Salvetree Green
Wich
Polstead Heath
Overbury Hall
Leyham
Cadman Hall
Green Upper Nurstead
Callis Street
Park Farm
Stone Street
White Street Green
Masons Bridge
Averly Hall
Payton Hall
Hagmoor Green
Rev. Mr. Gurdon Hall
Asington Vicarage
Lower Nurstead
Green
Asington
Wm. Beale Brand Esq.
Shelley
61
Polstead Green
Marshalls Green
Honor Bridge
Polstead
Shelley Hall
Leaden Hall
Giffords Hall
Sir J. Mannock
Gedding Hall
Bull Street
Stoke Hough
Withermarsh Green
Scotland Hall
Darking Tye
60
Leaden Heath
Stoke
Scotland Street
Beauchamps
Tendring Hall
Lady Rowley
Thorington Street
High Trees
Higham Marsh
59
Higham
Wiston Grange
NEYLAND
Stra
58
Wiston
Hall
Small Bridge

E

Elmset
Elmset Green
Flowton
Sycamore House
Bramford Tye
Bramford Hall
Nath. Acton Esq.
Bulling Green
Mock Beggars Hall
Thurlston
Chapel
Sparrows Nest
Whitton
Whitton White House
Deal Hall
Bramford
L I B E R
Hintlesham Priory
Aldham
Flowton Brook
Sproughton
Boss Hall
Claude Tonnereau
Burstall Green
Burstall
Hintlesham
Rich. Savage Lloyd Esq.
Sproughton
Sir Rob. Harland
Metcalfe Russel
O F
Stone Lodge
I P S W
Stoke Hall
Stoke
Washbrook
Chattisham Hall
Chattisham
Chattisham Place
Amer Hall
Hill House
Gusford Hall
Nova Scotia
Pond Hill
Farce Hall
Mace Green
White Elm
Copdock
Belstead Hall
Belstead
Spring Wood
Bourn Bridge
Bourn Hall
Thorington Hall
Wherstead
Wherstead Hall
Kings Green
S A M F O R D
Park House
Wherstead Heath
Raydon Hall
Raydon
Wenham Parva
Hall
Old Hall
Pale Pond Corner
Freston
Parsonage
Wenham Mag
Churchford
Wenham Priory
Capel
Bentley
Stalls Valley
Cutlers Wood
Shrub Corner
Shrub Wood
Bonds Hall
Wenham Place
Wenham Hill
Cross Green
Industry
Holton
Tattingston Hall
Tattingston
Woodly Wood
Hales
Grove
Hulley Wood
Martins Hills
Coppy
Dodnash Wood
H U N D R E
T. White Esq.
Js. Sewell Esq.
Holbrook
Burkets
Dodnash House or Priory
East
Eastbergholt
Bergholt Heath
Stratford
Ant. Dean Esq.
Park
Stutton
Holbrook Sluice
Brantham
Brantham Hall
Mr. Gaunt
Creping Hall
Crow Hall
Queech Farm
Stutton Hall
Flatford Mill
Judas Gap
Cattawade Bridges
New Mill
MANINGTREE
25

Culpho
Hall
Culpho Hall
Great Bealings
Hall Sir John Henniker Bar.t
Tuddenham
Playford
Little Bealings
Sparrows Nest
Green
Westerfield
Geo. Thomas Esq.
H.y Collet Esq.r
Martlesham Creek
Sluice
The Red House
M. Edgar Esq.r
Folly
Rushmere Hall
Rushmere
Martlesham
Hall
Great Boughton
Round Wood
Kesgrave
Martlesham Heath
Rushmere Heath
IPSWICH
Foxhall Heath
Foxhall
Waldringfield
Chilton Hall
Brightwells Plantation
Race Ground
Barley Decoy
Warren House
Turrells Hall
M. Maber
Brightwell
Brightwell Hall
Newbourn
Pardis
Hemley Hall
Hemley
Foxhall Heath
Bucklesham
Seven Hills
C O L N E I S
Nacton Heath
Nacton Industry House
Levington Heath
Kembroke
Kirkton Brook
Freston
Freston Tower
Parsonage
Orwell Park
Nacton
Earl of Hughbrooke
Philip Broke Esq.
Levington
Kirkton Green
Kirkton
Trimley
Faulkenham
Woolverston
W. Berners Esq.
ORWELL RIVER
Fen Mill
Stratton Hall
Marsh Farm
Hill Farm
Heath
Sir Charles Kent
Hall
Chelmondiston
Cowton Common
Lower Street
St. Martins
St. Marys
Renee Park
Old chapel now down
Grimston Hall
Candlett Farm
Crouch House
Shotley Hall
Shotley
Trimlies
Harkstead
Parsonage
Taylors Lane
Old Hall
Scrogs Farm
Parsonage
Holton Green
Nimbletons Corner
Blowfields Farm
Beaumonds Hall
Arwarton
Creek House
Shotley Gate
Cades Farm
Langar Common
STOUR RIVER
HARWICH
Langar Fort

Bredfield
Ufford
Melton
Bromswell
Wilford Bridge
WOODBRIDGE
Eyke
Rendlesham
Wantesden
Chillesford
Friday Street
Stavender Park
Butley
Tangham Walks
Tangham
Sutton Walks
WILFORD
Hollesly Heath
Boyton Heath
Capel
Boyton
Sutton
Shottisham
Hollesley
River Deben
HUNDRED
Ramsholt
Alderton
Bawdsey
Kirkton
Faulkenham
Walton
Felixstow
THE BA

Snape
Park Farm
O M E S G A T E
Rook Yard
Friston Decoy
Haslewood in Ruins
Snape Abby
Snape Bridge
Snape Common
Warren Ho.
The Mear
The River Alde
Iken Wood
Iken
Iken Decoy
Aldeburgh Hall
ALDBOROUGH
Heath
Iken Hall
Iken Com.
Corporation Marshes
Aldborough Quay
Laver of Ashes
Scudgrove Wood
Cowton House
Faceborns Bottom
Cutmore Wood
N D R E D
O
Sudborn Common
Smoaky House
Chillesford Decoy
Earl of Hetford
Sudborn Hall
Sudborn
Lanthorn Marshes
Chillesford Lodge
Butley River
Newton
ORFORD
Castle
Raydon
Fleet
Orford Key
Lights
Gedgrave
High House
Gedgrave Low House
Stone Ditch
Beach
Orford Ness
Ferry Sluice
Boyton Dock
Havergate
Salts
Beach
THE BAY

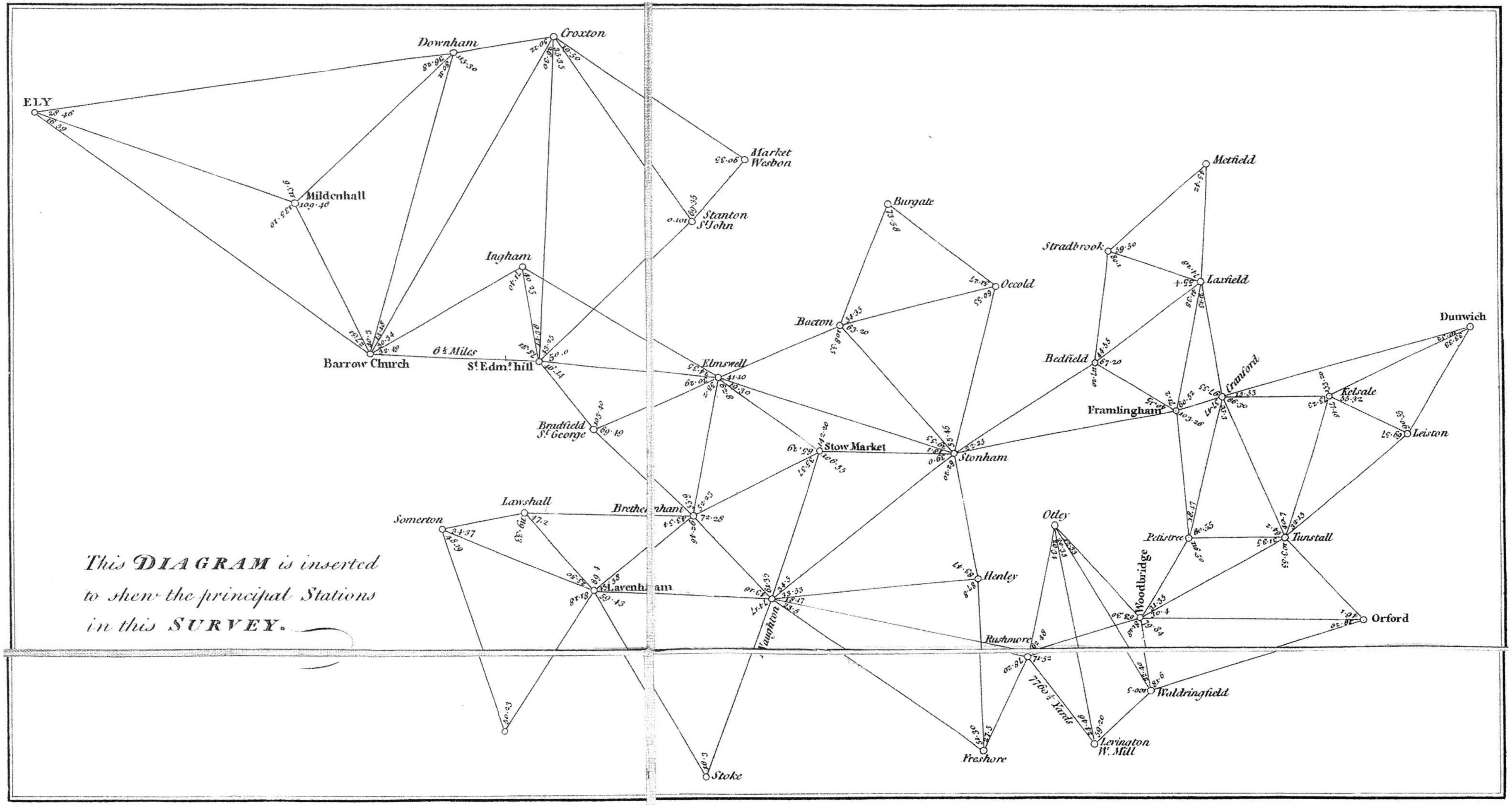

Triangulation diagram

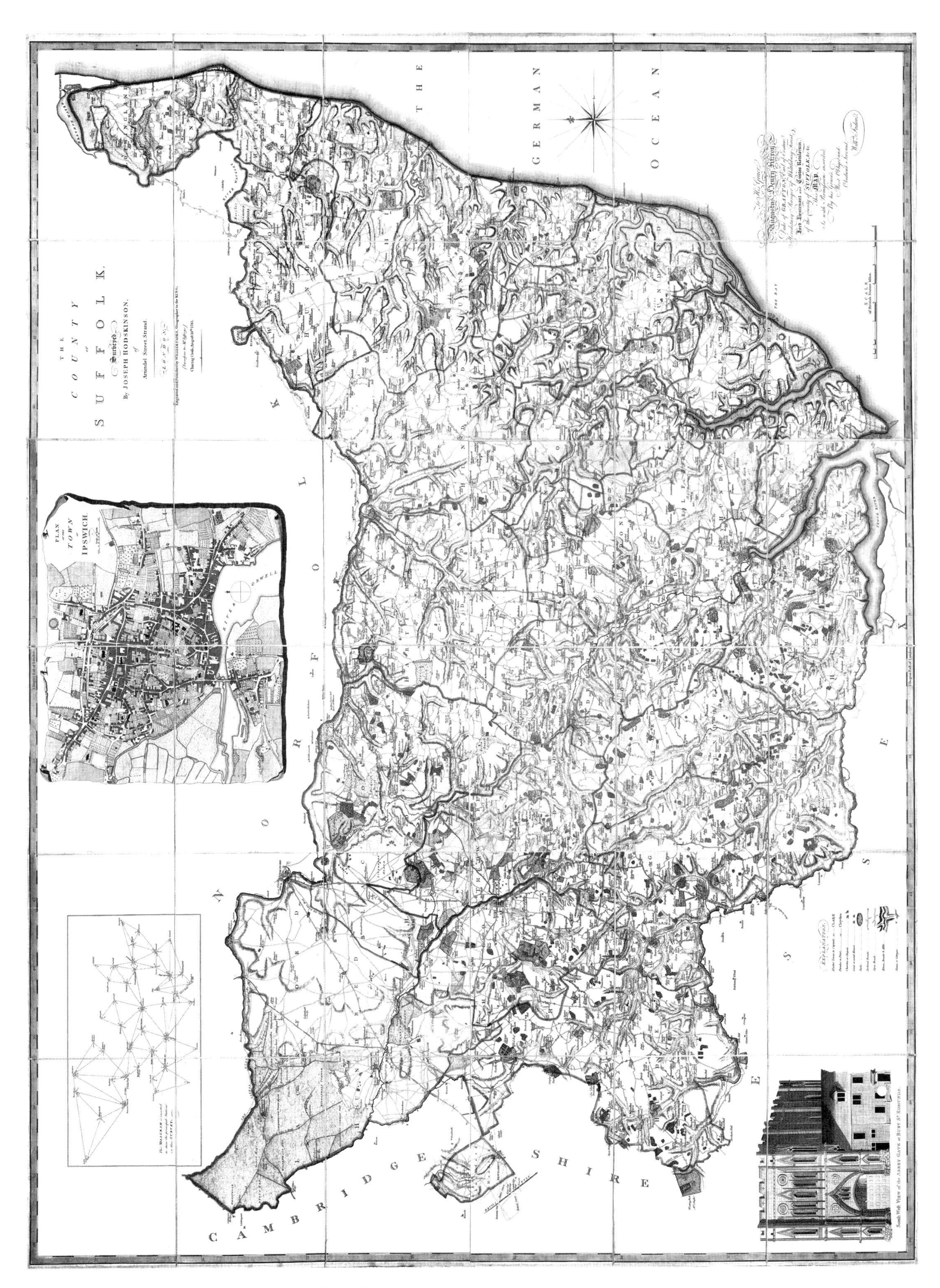

The six sheets of the original map

Also available from the Larks Press

Faden's Map of Norfolk in 1797
Introduction by J.C. Barringer

Bryant's Map of Norfolk in 1826
Introduction by J.C. Barringer

A Popular Guide to Norfolk Place-names
James Rye

A Popular Guide to Suffolk Place-names
James Rye

Weathervanes of Norfolk and Suffolk
Patricia Mockridge

And many other titles. Our full catalogue may be seen on our website
www.booksatlarkspress.co.uk.